BY MICHAEL GERBER

RESIDENT ALIENS

My close encounter of the best kind.

In 1977 my family moved from St. Louis to Jefferson City, so my father could work as a photographer for an HBCU, Lincoln University of Missouri. I was genuinely happy for my Dad, but I did not see why I had to come along.

"Mom, we've always been straight with each other," I said. "I think moving is a terrible idea."

"Michael, we're a family, and families make sacrifices for each other."

"So why can't you guys sacrifice by leaving me here?"

Exasperating. I was an exasperating child, for sure—but Mom and I both knew we barely fit into the bohemian Central West End, Rural Missouri would be like another planet. She and Dad drank and smoked—*openly*—and I was so verbal and adult-like I unnerved most people, including myself.

But my mother, slave to custom that she was, insisted that I, her only child, live with her. And so just like that, we exchanged an apartment that looked like the set of *The Thin Man* for an old, drafty, roach-infested house right behind the Missouri State Penitentiary, which to this day strikes me as the only defensible reason to live in Jeff City.

We rolled into town a few days after my eighth birthday, accompanied by a heat wave, and a "once-in-a-century" grasshopper infestation. Have you ever had a grasshopper fly into your mouth? Marvelous, can't recommend it highly enough. And these things weren't your pinky-sized lightweights; they had *heft*. Four inches long, yellow and black, flying, "tobacco-spitting" grasshoppers or, as the Bible calls them, "locusts." You'd think we'd have gotten the message; then again, we weren't Christians, only Catholic.

There simply wasn't much to do in Jefferson City, besides run from grasshoppers and wonder how things had gone so wrong so quickly. So I filled that summer before third grade by being terrified all the time. I read books about sharks and Bigfoot, naturally, and ghosts and UFOs. The only thing I liked about Jeff City was that it seemed like a place you really *could* get abducted by aliens.

Every Saturday, I walked down the hill to the library and plundered their small section of the paranormal. My reading habits made me a minor celebrity to the staff; I remember one young librarian checking out my copy of Jacques Valleé's *Journey to Magonia*. "Did you know the new Spielberg movie is based on this? I can't wait to see it." Librarians are cool.

Not so the mother of my new friends John and Benji; their house was halfway up the hill, a convenient place to put down my backpack full of terror and pick the locusts out of my hair. I liked her; she was kind and generous with the Kool Aid, and seemed slightly scared herself. I remember her actually fondling the cross around her neck as she examined *Chariots of the Gods*. "How can you believe such nonsense?" Then: "What's so funny, Mike? Why are you laughing?"

As resident aliens, we felt a certain obligation to signal to others of our kind, so we all might gather together for leisure and protection. Cocktail hour was established, and every day around five, we'd head out to the porch, the jazz and Steely Dan cranked up loud enough for passersby to hear. If some blue nose paused in disapproval, Dad would toast them with an open can of Busch.

A few kindred spirits did come: Neil was a journalist from Alabama covering the Capitol down the street, and his wife Mary Kaye worked at Lincoln. My science teacher, who shall remain nameless, used to share joints on our porch, detailing plans to run the fifth-grade football team like the Dallas Cowboys. Mom and Dad hosted parties regularly; I wasn't allowed to come out until 10:30, when everything would stop and we'd all gather around a laughably small black-and-white to watch *Saturday Night Live*. Transmissions from the home planet.

Apart from resident aliens, I remember basically two types of people in Jeff City. There were people affiliated with Lincoln, mostly African-American kids busting their ass to try to learn stuff and build a better life. Then there were the white folks, often much better off, who were dubious of the whole idea of education. They seemed scared of it, as if a person could stumble on the wrong fact or read the wrong sentence, and a life of blissful Faith would fly—*whoosh*—right out the window.

My good liberal parents tried to engage, but this was useless. The white American Christian had just begun to hack liberalism with the "*I just feel*" gambit. No matter how absurd or destructive your belief, you can always defeat a liberal by saying, "Well, I *just feel*..." As good liberals, we must always see things from their perspective: *They just feel* non-Christians are going to Hell. *They just feel* the earth is flat. *They just feel* tackle football is good for fifth-graders. *They just feel Close Encounters* is the work of Satan. (That last one is true—there's nothing more broadening than travel.)

When my dad covered a sporting event on campus, he often took me with him. As he roamed the sidelines, I would squeeze into the bleach-

MICHAEL GERBER (@mgerber937) is Editor & Publisher of *The American Bystander*.

ers, a little pink face in a rollicking sea of brown. Lincoln wasn't big—the fieldhouse held 2,300—but the student section made up for it by becoming a single organism, clapping and chanting and even throwing boxes of popcorn in the air when the occasion called for it (frequently). I can still hear that special *zing-zing-zing* when metal bleachers start to flex and vibrate, and civil engineers start to sweat.

As a person with cerebral palsy, Earth is rather dangerous for me, and sporting events are a great place to get knocked down, spilled on, trampled. But with those kids, I felt safe, protected. Looking back, I know there are historical reasons why a group of young African-Americans, a lot of them from the rural South, might've treated a little white boy with extra care. But collegians often look out for younger kids—it's one of the things I like the most about them.

Hanging with the athletes was even better than the students. To them, I was "Lil' Greg," Greg being my dad's name.

The varsity quarterback has special status on every college campus, and Lincoln's looked every inch the legend: he had a gold tooth and wore a blue bandana under his helmet. He was known as "Dr. Bad Butter," which is what I called him, too, once when he came over to the sidelines during practice.

"Nice juke, Dr. Bad Butter."

Butter cracked up. "You hear what Lil' Greg just said?" His voice was straight out of Mississippi. Butter slapped me five. "You awright, Lil' Greg."

"Butter! Quit screwing around!" That was the coach, whose smart, beautiful daughter was my babysitter. Butter trotted away, and received a gentle reaming about ball security. I wanted to make an excuse for my friend—to a kid like Butter, Jeff City was a metropolis. Maybe he felt like an alien, too. Dad nodded no. "Let Butter do his job, Mikey. You go sit over there."

Checking my ass for grasshoppers, I plopped down in the hot August sun. I loved it all—the grunting and the yelling, the clanking of the sleds, the popping of the pads, the cheers when a play worked, the swearing when it didn't. I liked the football guys; in another body, I would've been a football guy, myself. To me, Butter and his pals seemed like Supermen…even if they did go 6-7.

At Lincoln, it was the basketball team who *were* Supermen, at least for a year.

Lincoln had gotten to the Division II tournament for three years straight, and when the fall 1977 season rolled around, everyone knew it was going to be special—mainly because of two seniors: a surgical ball-distributor named Tim Abney, and a silky smooth scorer named Harold Robertson.

"LOOK SERIOUS, MIKEY": *Tim Abney (L), Harold Robertson (R) and me, 1977.*

The season began, and these two went to work, both special talents, each complementing the other. Tim and Harold were players you feel in the tips of your fingers, the ends of your hair. I felt it in the old Chicago Stadium, watching Jordan and Pippen, but in a small college gym it's an out-of-body experience.

As the victories mounted and the tournament came into view, everyone gave a little extra. Even the cheerleaders dropped the usual cheers and started making up their own. God, what I'd give for a full list, but I still remember a couple. One was a standard taunt:

"Pork chop, pork chop
Greasy, greasy
We can beat your team
Easy, easy!"

Stylish and catchy, but nothing compared to the masterpiece they sang, with syncopated claps, whenever a Lincoln player got whistled for a foul:

"That's all right, [Harold, etc]
We know you didn't mean it
Forget it
We'll talk about it later!"

I wish I could tell you that the Blue Tigers won it all—but that's not how this planet works. In the Elite Eight they were knocked out by Wisconsin-Green Bay. ("*Fucking* Wisconsin-Green Bay," as Neil and Dad let me say after.) To cheer me up, that weekend Mom took me to see *Close Encounters of the Third Kind*. The parts with soldiers and the government were scary, but the aliens were cool, except when they smiled.

I'm happy to report that Tim Abney and Harold Robertson still live and thrive. Harold, Lincoln's greatest scorer, was drafted in the first round by the Lakers; I can only imagine his adventures on Planet Los Angeles circa 1978. And Tim, Lincoln's greatest point guard, became the team's assistant coach. Years later, he ran Lincoln's athletics department.

In the last practice before the tournament, Dad asked Tim and Harold to pose for this picture, and they graciously agreed. "Put your hand on Harold's shoulder, Mikey." Touching them made me feel giddy, like touching the side of a rocket. I kept smiling; Dad asked for one serious take, "in case that's funnier."

When I look at this photo today, remembering how nice these young men were, how talented; knowing how rough life can be, and how much luck you need just to survive; thinking of young black men, ever treated like aliens in their own country… When I look at this photo today, *I just feel.* B

TABLE OF CONTENTS

More Art Bots on page 49

DEPARTMENTS

GALLIMAUFRY

SHORT STUFF

The AMERICAN
BYSTANDER
Founded 1981 by Brian McConnachie
#22 • Vol. 6, No. 2 • June 2022

EDITOR & PUBLISHER
Michael Gerber
HEAD WRITER Brian McConnachie
SENIOR EDITOR Alan Goldberg
ORACLE Steve Young
STAFF LIAR P.S. Mueller
INTREPID TRAVELER Mike Reiss
EAGLE EYES Patrick L. Kennedy
TWOFIFTYONE.NET Chase/Doyle/Nink
AGENTS OF THE 2ND BYSTANDER INT'L
Eve Alintuck, Melissa Balmain, Ron Barrett, Roz Chast, Rick Geary, Sam Gross
MANAGING EDITOR EMERITA
Jennifer Finney Boylan
CONSIGLIERA Kate Powers
COVER BY Chitty

ISSUE CONTRIBUTORS
Lila Ash, Mat Barton, Barry Blitt, George Booth, Pat Boyle, Calef Brown, Tom Chitty, Adam Cooper, Drew Dernavich, Bob Eckstein, Ivan Ehlers, Noell Wolfram Evans, Derek Evernden, Emily Flake, E.R. Flynn, Rich Frost, James Finn Garner, Roman Genn, Gregory Gerber, Ilana Gordon, Alex Griffiths, Bruce Handy, Lance Hansen, Quentin Hardy, Ron Hauge, Bruce Handy, Michel Jedinak, John Jonik, Victor Juhasz, Joe Keohane, Varun Khadpe, Ken Krimstein, Stan Mack, Ross MacDonald, Arthur Meyer, Oliver Ottitsch, Michael Pershan, K.A. Polzin, Zak Pullen, Anthony Russo, Anthony Scibelli, Jim Siergey, Dalton Vaughn, Evan Waite, D. Watson, Bill Woodman, Steve Young & Jonathan Zeller.

Lanky Bareikis, Jon Schwarz, Laura Sweet, Alleen Schultz, Diane Gray & Molly Bernstein, Joe Lopez, Ivanhoe & Gumenick, Greg & Trish Gerber, Kelsey Hoke.
NAMEPLATES BY Mark Simonson
ISSUE CREATED BY Michael Gerber

FEATURES

OUR BACK PAGES

CARTOONS & ILLUSTRATIONS BY

Victor Juhasz, Gregory Gerber, Barry Blitt, George Booth, Sam Gross, Bill Woodman, Bob Eckstein, Dalton Vaughn, Ross MacDonald, Lance Hansen, Emily Flake, D. Watson, Drew Dernavich, Calef Brown, Marques Duggans.

Sam's Spot

"After he poops we have to leave immediately. It's radioactive."

COVER

TOM CHITTY has a whole world inside his head, and it was my very great pleasure to help him let some of it out on our cover (and via "Art Bots" as well). Tom, please tell us you're really working on the screenplay for *Spiderman Vs. Jaws*—that's a movie I'd camp out for.

ACKNOWLEDGMENTS

 The following material has previously appeared, and is reprinted here with permission of the author(s): Roman Genn's Putin illustration originally appeared in *The New Republic* magazine. The photos used on pp. 46-47 are from Unsplash.com.

THE AMERICAN BYSTANDER, *Vol. 6, No. 2*, (978-0-578-28364-7). Publishes ~4x/year. ©2022 by Good Cheer LLC. No part of this magazine can be reproduced, in whole or in part, by any means, without the written permission of the Publisher. For this and other queries, email Publisher@americanbystander.org, or write: Michael Gerber, Publisher, *The American Bystander*, 1122 Sixth St., #403, Santa Monica, CA 90403. Single copies can be purchased at www.americanbystander.org/store. **Subscribe at www.patreon.com/bystander.** Other info—probably more than anyone could possibly require—can be found on our website, www.americanbystander.org. Thankee for reading.

LET THE MATH GAMES BEGIN!

MORE THAN 70 COMPETITIVE CHALLENGES, PERFECT FOR GROUP OR SOLO PLAY

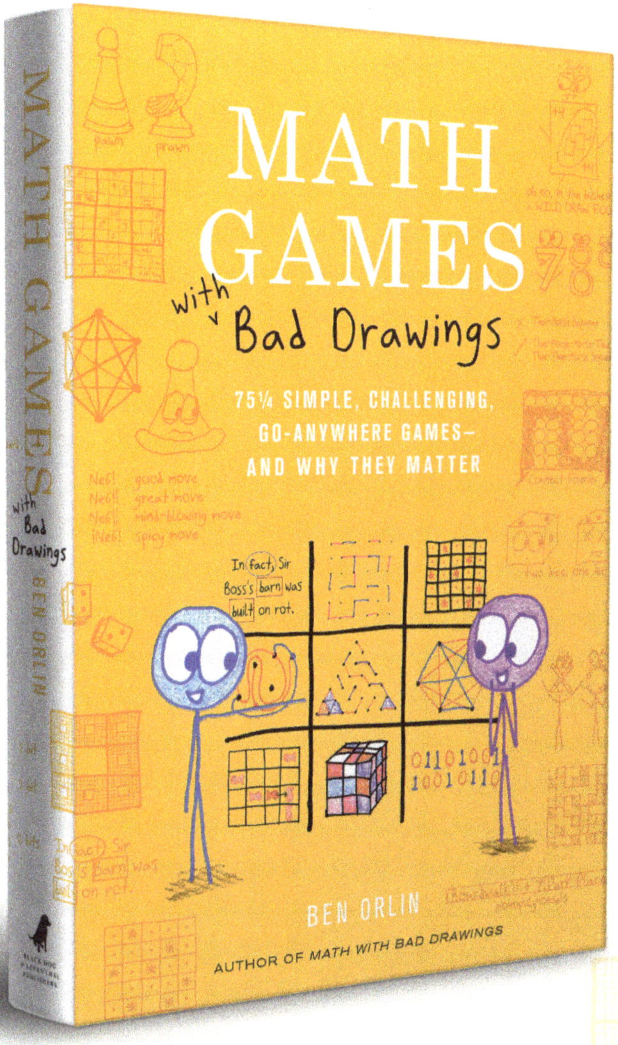

PERFECT FOR FAMILY GAME PLAY, OR SOLO CHALLENGES.

INCLUDES:

- ULTIMATE TIC-TAC-TOE
- SPROUTS
- BATTLESHIP
- QUANTUM GO FISH
- DOTS AND BOXES
- ORDER AND CHAOS
- SEQUENCIUM
- CATS AND DOGS
- *AND DOZENS MORE*

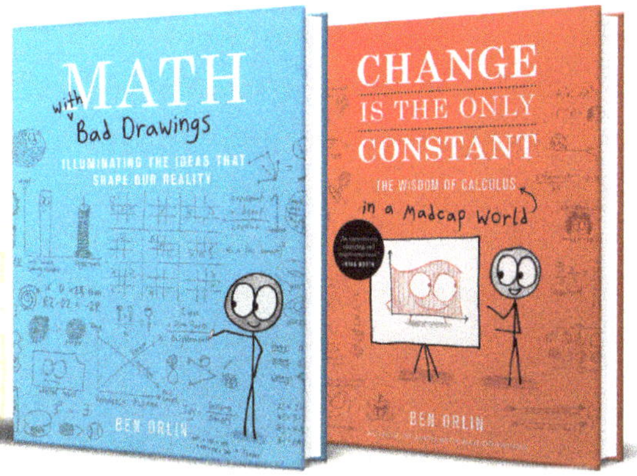

"I'm loving this math book with puzzles. Such a gentle, playful way to teach these abstract concepts. Like a pill pocket for math!"

— Allie Brosh,
bestselling author of *Hyperbole and a Half*

ON SALE APRIL 5, 2022 | @MATHWITHBADDRAWINGS | IN HARDCOVER AND EBOOK WHEREVER BOOKS ARE SOLD

BLACK DOG & LEVENTHAL PUBLISHERS

CIRCE, THE WITCH WHO TURNED SAILORS INTO PIGS, LUSTED AFTER **PICUS**, THE SON OF SATURN. ONE DAY SHE DISGUISED HERSELF AS A PHANTOM BOAR TO LURE PICUS FROM HIS HUNTING PARTY. AFTER SHE REVEALED HERSELF, PICUS SPURNED HER AMOROUS ADVANCES SO CIRCE PUNISHED HIM BY CHANGING HIM INTO A *WOODPECKER!* HIS WIFE **CANENS**, KNOWN FOR HER BEAUTIFUL SINGING VOICE THAT EVEN ENTHRALLED THE ANIMALS OF THE FOREST, SEARCHED FUTILELY FOR PICUS UNTIL, WITH BROKEN HEART, DROWNED HERSELF IN THE TIBER RIVER.

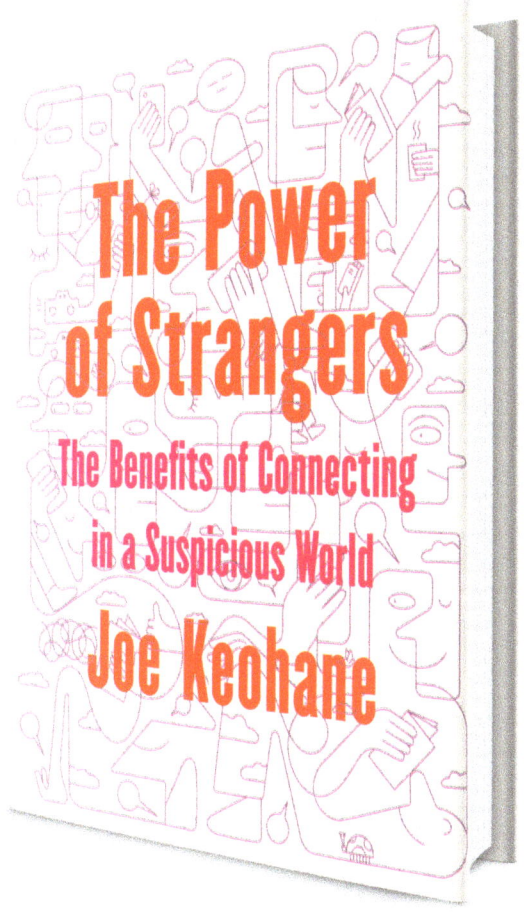

BY STAFF

BILL WOODMAN, 1936-2022

Bystander's *original Comics Editor died suddenly on February 12. Here are a few words from his colleagues.*

I got to know Bill in his Portland, Maine years—a bunch of cartoonists in the appropriately-small Maine cartooning community used to get together a couple times a year. That evolved into Mike Lynch and my visiting Bill once a month and hanging out in his one-room apartment, which was filled with his art and notebooks and scraps of ideas taped all over the walls. He would always greet me at the door with "Have you sold anything to *The New Yorker*, John?"

Bill, Mike, Dave Jacobson, the late Jeff Pert and I (which constituted a quorum of the Maine cartoonists' community) put out a book of Maine-themed cartoons (*see below*), and various configurations of us would have book signings around the state. Bill gave me guided tours of his hometown, Bangor, and he knew every backroad diner in the state. ("Take a left up here, John, there's a good place to get a sandwich.")

For a couple months pre-pandemic we started going to a local mall and drawing—it was Bill's idea—and eating mall Chinese food. He always had a piece of scrap paper in his pocket and an idea for a gag or children's book.

The only good thing about Bill's passing is that I'll never have to eat at Denny's again...he loved that senior menu.

—John Klossner

Bill was part of the group I became part of when I first came to New York back in the 1980s, to peddle my wares in person at *The New Yorker*. "Look Day" at Lee Lorenz's office was around 11 a.m. on Wednesdays; afterwards many of us went to lunch together at a neighborhood restaurant. Sam Gross, Jack Ziegler, Roz Chast, and another dozen or so of my heroes were in attendance, including Bill.

We would show each other our rejects and exchange comments and, from the older guys, advice. It was Bill who I recall making reference to a quote from, I think, James Dickey, referring to the blank piece of paper we all confront whenever we sit down to draw or write as a "Blazing White Island." He certainly knew how to fill that island with great cartoon ideas. I was very sorry to hear of his passing.

—Mick Stevens

Bill Woodman is a great cartoonist and one of the funniest "draw-ers" of all time, right up there with George Booth. Back when we used to hang out together, he allowed me the privilege of looking over any number of the obsessive sketchbooks that were always within his easy reach, usually right there in one of the overlarge pockets of his surplus Air Force overcoat. They were filled with casual observations, preliminary ideas for cartoons, and reprimands to himself about why he wasn't coming up with any good ideas on any particular day. Each page was chock full of bits and pieces that were wry, engaging, and all just plain funny to look at. I never had a better time looking at anything in my life. Why *The New Yorker* didn't use a ton more of his work over the years was a never-ending, mind-boggling mystery to me.

—Jack Ziegler, quoted on Michaelmaslin.com

At the time of his death, Bill was working on a book of condom-themed cartoons; I liked this one particularly. May your ascent be easy, Bill.

Bill and I worked together for over thirty years. We'd sit at opposite ends of the table at my apartment, or at his place, and we'd doodle and fill up pads of paper until one of us got a gag. Then we would doodle some more until the next gag emerged.When Bill moved to Maine we weren't able to do this anymore.

Bill had a quick mind and a very funny drawing style. He could tell a joke, and did so with a tremendous sense of freedom—his people were definitely not stiff. He had a unique talent and we worked well together.

He was a colleague, and a friend.

—Sam Gross **B**

“There’s a phrase of Bill’s that I think about almost every day. He called the blank sheet of paper on the drawing table “the blazing island of white.”

ROZ CHAST

BILL WOODMAN *photographed in his studio, August 2016, by friend and fellow cartoonist, Mike Lynch. Mike remembers, “Bill always smiled and said, ‘Drawing every day is a disease.’”*

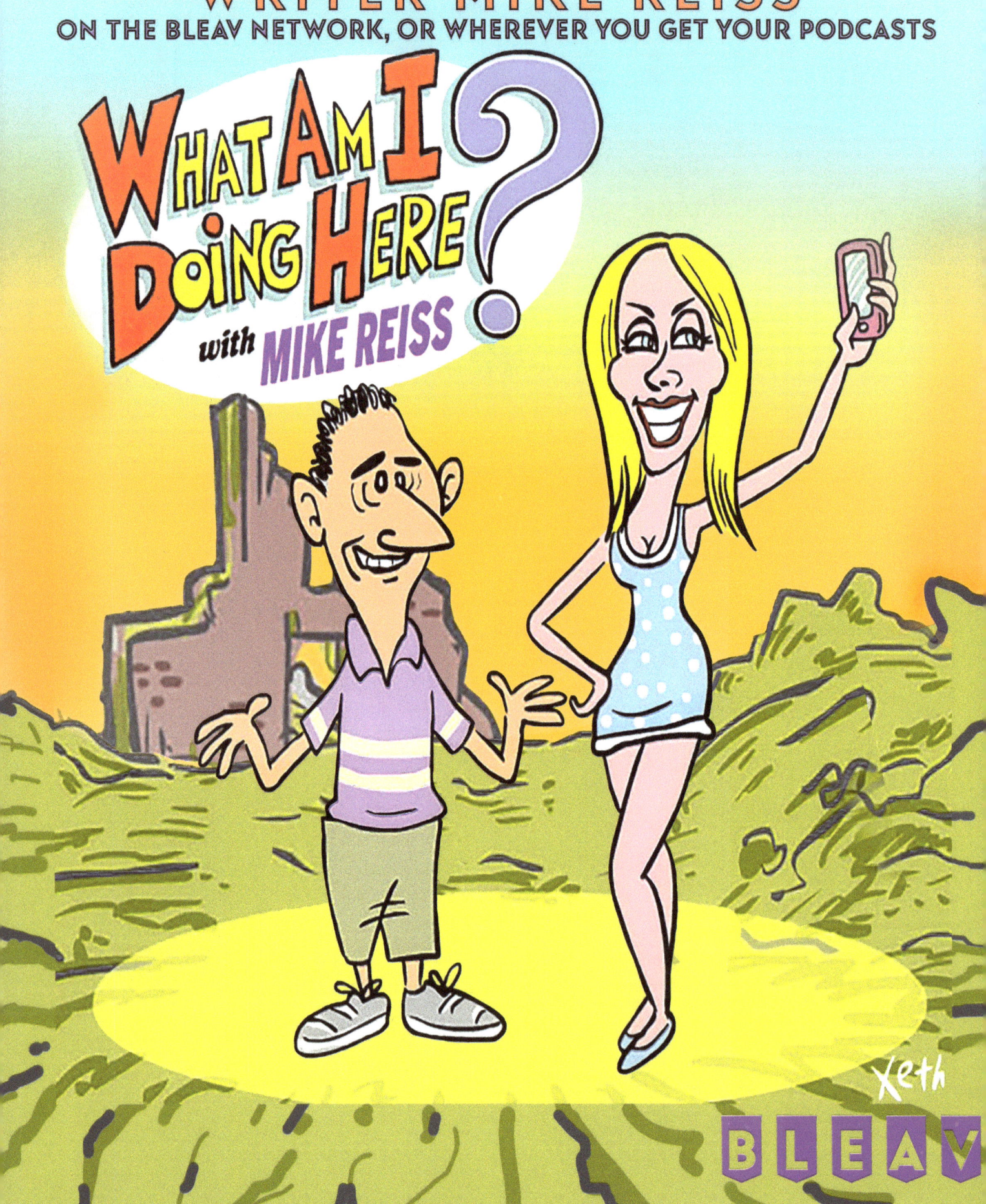

Gallimaufry

TODAY'S HEADLINES.

• GYRE WIDENING, OFFICIALS SAY
• REPORT: FALCONS CANNOT HEAR FALCONER
• ANARCHY LOOSED UPON WORLD
•"ROUGH BEAST" SLOUCHING TOWARDS BETHLEHEM—WHAT IT COULD MEAN FOR YOU

—Michael Pershan

WHO MURDERED BUN-BUN?

You spent all morning arranging the table with fake cupcakes and tea cups. You invited four stuffed animal friends that you love, and everyone at the tea party was having a great time. The conversation was lively, the plushies were vibing, and everyone was fake-nibbling macaroons. It was the event of the season.

That's when you excused yourself to go boom-boom, and returned to a scene of horror.

Your stuffed rabbit Bun-Bun, who moments earlier had been propped up in her chair sipping invisible tea, was knocked to the floor, dead. Her red ribbon had been stripped from her neck, so this was no accident. One of the other guests must have killed her. *But who?*

THE SUSPECTS

Guest #1: **Mr. Bear**

Mr. Bear is the snuggliest bear of all time. He has adorable ears and gives the best hugs. At the crime scene, he had a rose between his paws, which suggests that he was in love with one of the guests. Did Bun-Bun break his heart? Was this a lover's quarrel that spun dangerously out of control?

Guest #2: **Froggy**

Though she kept this secret, you know that Froggy had done time in a Goodwill bin with other unwanted toys, Sharpie-scrawled Raggedy Anns and racist Golliwogs. She'd lived a hard life on the inside, and it showed: One of her eyes drooped and she had stuffing coming out of her side. Froggy had been lucky to make it out alive, and would do just about anything to keep from going back. Did Bun-Bun see something she shouldn't have?

Guest #3: **Stitch**

Former Disney star Stitch was once on top of the animated world; back in the day he could have any Pikachu he wanted, and wherever he went, kids knew his name. But he'd fallen on hard times after Lilo left—Stitch's solo films tanked, and his ill-conceived rap album made him the laughingstock of the Disney family. Cast aside as a has-been, he started doing drugs. Pretty soon the money dried up. Had Bun-Bun been killed in a robbery gone wrong?

In the course of my investigation, I interviewed each of the suspects in turn:

Something about his big dumb grin told me that **Mr. Bear** was unlucky in love. After all, showing up at a tea party with a rose is a real cuck move. I tried to delve deeper into his romantic history, but he refused to talk. Or move. Or blink.

Froggy showed a chilling lack of emotion over Bun-Bun's murder. All she said when I pulled her string was, "*I'm so hoppy!*" Given this glimpse into her warped psyche, Froggy jumped to the top of my list of suspects. Jumped like frog wordplay.

When I pressed his belly for answers, **Stitch** just moved his arms and legs up and down, as a Hawaiian song from his first movie played. He was clearly trying to impress me, but I gave it to him straight-up: "*Lilo & Stitch* is mid-tier Disney at best." He went silent after that.

That evening, I got a tip—there had been a nanny-cam! What I saw shocked me: Approximately nine seconds after you left to go potty, your dog Peaches sauntered in and snatched Bun-Bun out of her chair, ripping the victim's ribbon off in the process!

When I apprehended Peaches on his dog bed, he was in possession of the ribbon, so I had him dead to rights. But I wanted the confession. During his interrogation, I asked if he had committed the crime, and he barked once for yes.

Case closed.

—Evan Waite

WHAT'S IN A NAME?

by Ivan Ehlers

APRIL FOOLS.

Each year they do the same damn thing:
bulbs bloom and start to glow,
then—whammo! Sayonara, spring!—
a cold snap knocks them low.
You'd think by now they'd finally learn
to wait a week or three
until the risk of freezer burn
is gone, but no sirree:
come April, come a hint of sun,
they'll pop back up for sure,
to make it seem that winter's done—
and sucker us once more.

—Melissa Balmain

COVID BY THE DECADES: A RETROSPECTIVE VIEW.

Ages 0-10: "The grownups are scared!"
Ages 10-20: "I can't see my friends."
Ages 20-30: "What life? My launch is stalled."
Ages 30-40: "These kids are driving me nuts."
Ages 40-50: "My career is fucked."
Ages 50-60: "Just when I was free of my kids, they're back."
Ages 60-70: "My retirement is fucked."
Ages 80-90: "I hope I survive buying groceries."
Ages 90-99: "I'll never live to be 100."
Ages 70-80: "Whoo-hoo! There will be plenty of room at the nursing homes!"
Fucking Boomers win again.

—Quentin Hardy

THINGS YOU CAN GET HIGH ON.

Marijuana
Methamphetamine
Psilocybe cubensis mushrooms
MDMA
LSD and other ergot derivatives
Ketamine
Bath salts
Morning Glory seeds
Life *(unconfirmed)*

—Hart Bibble

CARRAW!

"Oh, no—I think a crow is having a medical emergency!" my cohabitant calls to me as she waves me over to the window.

I join her windowside and listen. A bird-murdering sound is coming from the street. "It sounds like a crow or crows are being throttled. Like someone

"I can feel my goth phase coming on."

is strangling a minimum of one crow."

"Poor thing. What can we do?"

"Nothing. Anyone who would strangle a crow or crows is unpredictable. Not to be confronted. Is the door locked?"

We both grab at the handle, make sure the door is secured.

The next morning, walking the pup, I see a neighbor. "Did you hear that crow being murdered yesterday?" I inquire. "Or crows?"

"A murder of crows?" he says, then appears to think. "Oh, you must mean the Amazon delivery van."

I sense that I will soon feel foolish.

"It's their *beep-beep-beep*," he says. "So when the Amazon van reverses, instead of beeping, it makes a noise like a crow in distress. Or a dying chicken."

"And this is considered an improvement?"

"By someone. Or a panel of someones."

The solution to the mystery is so asinine that I don't feel foolish. I'm too happy for the crows.

Later, at home, I pass the intel on to my cohabitant.

"I lost sleep over this," she says, "thinking about that poor crow being strangled."

"There was no crow."

"So you said. Still, sleep was lost."

We're no complainers, but urged on, I make a call to Amazon. I reach a "Jane" (cannot be her real name), who needs my order number and a description of the problem. I try to explain about the van, the hated reversing noise, the tormented not-crow, but this is off Jane's script—she really needs an order number. I feel bad for involving her, tell her never mind.

Later, during lunch, the loathsome sound returns, drawing us away from our sandwiches and to the window. We locate the van, which caws piteously as it positions itself for deliveries. Then the driver hops out, runs a package to our stoop, hits the buzzer, and sprints back to the van.

"*Carraw, Carraw!*" the van screeches, then pulls out and away.

I retrieve the package, bring it inside. My cohabitant opens it. It's batteries.

"Finally," she says.

—*K.A. Polzin*

LIFE: THE FAQ.

We're glad that you are considering Life. Before you decide if Life is right for you, please check out some of our FAQ's.

What is Life?

The period of time between when you are born and when you die.

When am I born?

When you are born.

What happens in Life?

Problems, jumping, books, learning the disappearing thumb trick thing, hearing the song "Love Shack" at a wedding and getting surprisingly into it, shampoo, etc.

What do you have to do to continue being alive?

Simply don't die.

Oh. So Life is easy?

No, it is the hardest thing you will ever do.

Do twins count as one person or two?

Two.

What else happens in Life?

Darts, water, cocaine, math, Wendy's, blinking, YouTube trampoline fails, secrets, etc.

What should I do if I accidentally put my AirPods in the washer?

Remove AirPods from case. Do not plug in within at least 12 hours of exposure to water.

What is the meaning of Life?

TBD.

Does anything else happen in Life that you didn't previously mention?

Raisins, power, getting coffee with your cousin, blankets, tragedies, rice pilaf, etc.

When is Life over?

2052.

—*Arthur Meyer*

REJECTED BOND GIRL NAMES.

Ashley Trashcock
Vagina Holiday
Bobbi Catfish
Vanessa Sexual

—*Pat Boyle*

27 REASONS TO VOTE FOR SONNY PRICE.

Sonny Price is an extraordinary candidate.

"I'll see if we have some ginger ale."

He's your next-door neighbor and cares about you.

He used to own the Buick place on Park Street.

No, Frank had the Chevy place.

Sonny loves all animals and would make a great commissioner of fish and game.

Where did you hear that?

Sonny Price would never do that to an alpaca.

A llama maybe, but never an alpaca.

Vote Sonny Price!

He is not a necrophiliac!

Who said that?

Oh. Charlene. What a bitch.

Have you met her? Then don't tell me not to call her that.

They had a fling a while ago. Before the D-I-V-O-R-C-E.

Divorce. Do you know how to spell?

What do you mean you never heard about it?

The news spread across town faster than herpes in a hot rod.

Vote Sonny Price!

Though, some people say that he murdered somebody.

I shit you not.

Doreen—you know Doreen, always walking around with that white stick? She told me.

Because she *saw* him do it!

She is not blind!

Oh. That explains the white stick.

Bob Freeney? You'd vote for that asshole? One winter he was driving plow and took out my mailbox! Mail everywhere! And not just catalogs. Though there were some embarrassing catalogs in there.

You know, Bob could be a murdering necrophiliac.

Vote Sonny Price!

—Rich Frost

SMITTEN IN SPRING.

I yelled this morning at my son;
I criticized my spouse.
Ten minutes after I was done,
a hailstorm hit our house.
It pummeled the whole neighborhood—
chipped roofs, denuded trees,
stripped paint from metal, clay and wood,
concussed the chickadees.
A mile away, we later heard,
brief showers sifted down;
the only place the gods had stirred
was our small slice of town.
A next-door neighbor swigged her beer,
raked dogwood blooms aside
and mused aloud, "Why us? Why here?"
"Just rotten luck," I lied.

—Melissa Balmain

FROM THE DESK OF THE GODFATHER.

To those who paid me a personal visit in the parlor, I know I promised any favor on the day of my daughter's wedding. See my responses below.

- Don Francisco, I can read your screenplay but I can't give notes.
- Ricardo, you can borrow it, but I'll need it back in time for Halloween.
- Roberto, I can give a soft yes but I'll need to check with my podiatrist first.
- Dario, yes I do know Jane Fonda but frankly I'm uncomfortable passing that on.
- Little Martin, my sincere apologies but I forgot your question. Also, I broke your air fryer.
- Johnny Boy, my answer is yes. Always. But not on the Sabbath.
- Stefano, I think you have the wrong guy. You want Don Mattingly.
- Carmela, I'd love to help but I'm banned from practicing dentistry in this state.
- And Frank, for the last time, I'm not beating up Mr. Allen for you. That creep is like, five-six, tops. Do it yourself.

—Alex Griffiths

AGREE TO DISAGREE.

I guess we'll have to agree to disagree. You think I put a bear trap in the living room to hurt, I'm sorry, "maim" you.

MULE'S DINER
Stan Mack
ALEXA'S GRANNY DIED AND LEFT ALEXA HER DOG, WILLIAM H. MACY.
DOG ?
ALEXA FLEW TO FLORIDA TO PICK HIM UP.
I DIDN'T EVEN THINK SHE LIKED ME.
W.H.M. WAS THE UGLIEST, ANGRIEST ANIMAL ALEXA HAD EVER ENCOUNTERED.
YOUR GRANNY LOVED THAT DOG.
WILL
ALEXA TRIED TO LIKE HIM. BUT WILLIAM H. MACY WAS SO HORRIBLE, HE TERRIFIED EVERYONE..
FOR HER OWN SANITY, ALEXA DECIDED TO DO AWAY WITH W.H.M.
Hit man
No job too small.
10% off with this ad.
PENNY SAVER
THE HIT MAN PROVED HIS SKILL BY SHOOTING AN ARROW INTO:
THE WIND--AND THE WIND DIED,
THE RAIN--AND THE RAIN STOPPED,
THE WAVES--AND THE TIDE RAN OUT.
CONFIDENTLY, HE SHOT AT W.H.M., WHO GLARED AT THE ARROW. THE ARROW NEVER REACHED ITS TARGET.
THE ARCHER SHOT ALL HIS ARROWS. EACH SPED STRAIGHT AT W.H.M, YET NONE ARRIVED. THE HIT MAN LEFT, DEFEATED.
ALEXA GAVE UP.
WHAT TO DO WITH THE ANGRIEST DOG IN THE WORLD.
D. LYNCH
©2021 stanmack

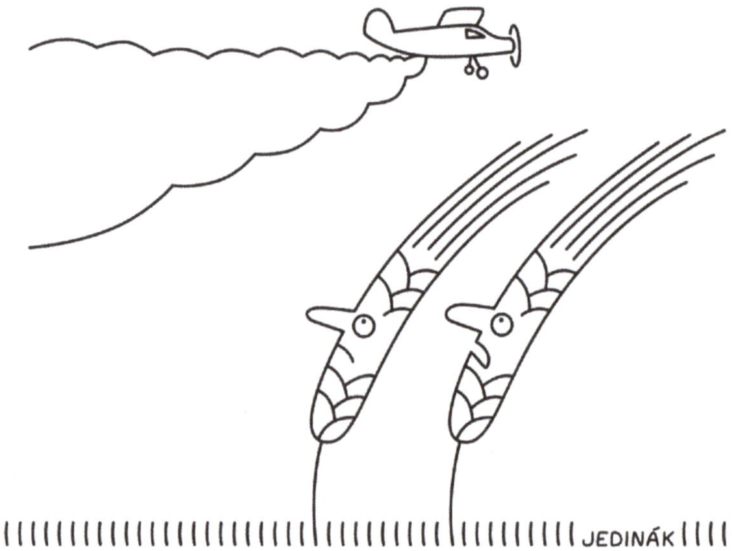

"Chemtrails. That's how they control us."

I say I put it there to catch any bears that wander in. Sorry for trying to keep you safe. What's next? Are you going to make me take down the anvil hanging in our bedroom? My *grandmother's* anvil? There just really is no pleasing you, is there?

—Noell Wolfram Evans

MINIATURE ADULTS.

I would never think twice about hitting a child. Unless there were two children, then I would think once per child.

—Varun Khadpe

THIS MAN, THIS MONSTER.

Some people thought Professor Darkwillow was a monster, because of his unethical experiments and their ghoulish consequences, but to me, it was because of the way he ate.

—Anthony Scibelli

PROSPECTORS.

This morning, we finished the last of the beef jerky. It was everyone's favorite. We're down to just the turkey and salmon jerkies. After those are done, we'll have to hope that we finally strike the gold we've been looking for so we can produce gold jerky.

—Jonathan Zeller

UNDERGROWTH.

The worst part of spring isn't pollen,
or sickly and trickly catarrh,
or the slippery petals soon fallen
on patio, driveway, and car.
I can live with the rains always plinking,
black mud and brown crud on my Keds,
and the hailstorms that, just when I'm thinking,
"Nice tulips!" come bomb them to shreds.
No, the horror of spring is recession:
when snow starts to go, the world's peeled;
April warmth brings an end to discretion
as tufts, long unmown, lie revealed.
I can feel myself blushing—will neighbors
catch sight of this blight, winter's dregs,
and be shocked at my slackening labors?
I sigh, and I go shave my legs.

—Melissa Balmain B

WARNING! WARNING! WARNING!
Much of this material first appeared on **twofiftyone.net**, *Bystander's* website for short stuff. It's edited by Adam Chase, Ben Doyle and Jonah Nink, and is POWERFULLY ADDICTIVE.

PETER KUPER

IN TER SECTS

Where Arthropods and Homo Sapiens Meet

Stephen A. Schwarzman Building
Rayner Special Collections Wing
Third Floor

January – August 13, 2022

New York Public Library

BY BOB ECKSTEIN

FINALLY, I'M A MODEL

One Weird Trick is making me a LOT of money

After a challenging couple of years, I've pivoted to an exciting new semi-retirement career: Clickbait Ad modeling! Turns out, I'm a natural, landing lucrative campaigns and making over 17 figures in the last year.

What's the secret to all my success? *Efficiency*. Below, I've reprinted a few recent ads, things you've probably clicked on yourself. Believe it or not, they all come from one photoshoot! See if you can tell.

Sponsored

This Miracle Fruit Will Cure Your ED

See Why This Man is in Jail the Rest of His Life

How Voting and Tipping Causes Cancer

8 Tell-Tale Signs He Is Cheating on You

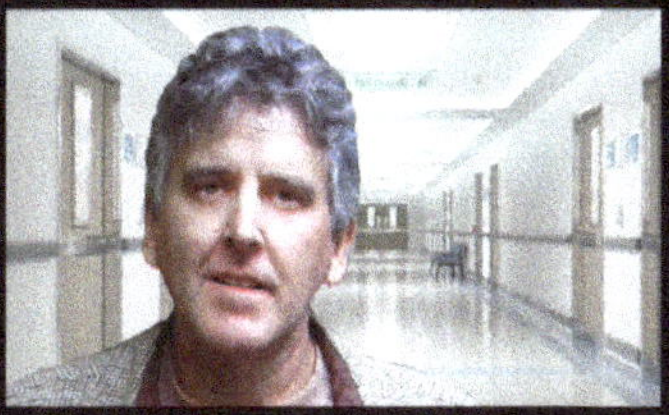

Do You Have a Dungeons & Dragons Addiction?

He Disappered 48 Years Ago with This Incredible Secret

Are You Married to a Deadbeat?

Powerful Herb So You Don't Have to Look Like This Man

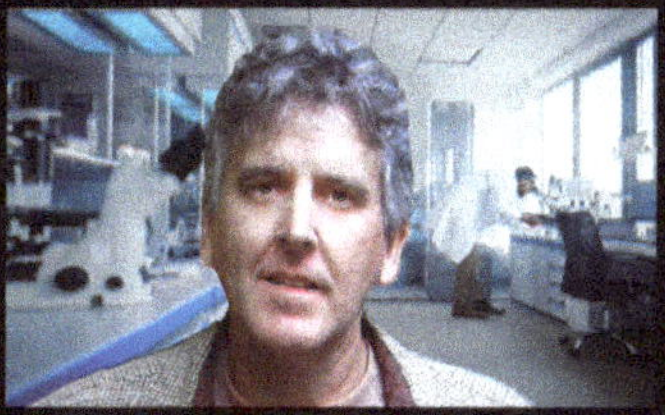

Our Brains Are Shrinking

Embarrassing Explosive Diarrhea? Eat More of This

Today's Toupees Are Undetectable

The Man Behind the World's Unsolved Art Thefts

B

BOB ECKSTEIN *is a* New York Times *bestselling illustrator and the world's leading snowman expert* (The Illustrated History of the Snowman). *He teaches writing and drawing at NYU.*

BY JOE KEOHANE

GONE TO THE DOGS!

How many emotional support dogs in the office is too many emotional support dogs in the office?

Dear Advice Annie,

I work in a small office of about twenty-five. Several weeks ago, one of my reports, I'll call him "Danny," started bringing his small bulldog Petra to work. We have no set policy on this, but Danny had been having a tough time readjusting to office life, so I thought if it helped him, it was worth the minor inconveniences of having a dog around every once in a while.

But then Danny began bringing Petra every day. He also brought in her bowl, a bed, toys, etc. When I tripped over her food dish, scattering kibble everywhere, Danny accused me of doing it on purpose. He said Petra was his "emotional support animal" and he'd take it up with our Head of People if I had a problem with it. As a progressive manager always eager to avoid a conflict, I said it was fine.

But then "Marcie" brought in her beagle. At first, I tried to make light of it in an email: "SUBJECT: Dog population up 100%!" But Marcie told me I was creating a toxic workplace, so I allowed that one too—even though the two dogs spent the workday barking at one another.

I figured that would be the end of it, but it was only the beginning.

Next, "Andy" brought in his own emotional support dog, a (poorly behaved) Jack Russell. Then "Samara" brought her enormous border collie. And "Andrea," my 22-year-old assistant, arrived with a fluffy little bichon in a duffle bag. Each came with their own accoutrements, all flashpoints for unrelenting conflict.

I attempted to impose a new rule concerning dogs in the office, but Andy and Samara threatened to go to the Head of People, and Andrea attacked me on Twitter for creating a "harmful work environment." When I took her aside and voiced a gentle exception, she grew furious and declared, "It isn't my job to educate you." So I relented, again, reminding myself of how privileged I am to not require an emotional support dog, and hoping the situation would improve.

It did not. Samara's border collie began herding staffers, nipping at our heels until it had us all tightly packed and trembling in a corner of the conference room. After chewing up the carpet, Andy's Jack Russell somehow got into the walls and managed to disable our internet, before chewing its way back down through the drop ceiling. Andrea's bichon—admittedly very cute—sparked a dark sexual energy between Danny's dog and Marcie's dog, who then spent half the time growling at one another and the other half rutting in the breakroom sink, pausing only long enough to snap at anyone who tried to retrieve their lunch from the refrigerator. That is, until the Jack Russell chewed through the cord, shocking himself into madness and permanently disabling the appliance.

Other staffers began bringing in dogs for protection. I could no longer keep track of what belonged to whom. Someone brought in a Doberman, which quickly turned on its owner and formed a sado-masochistic sexual triangle with Danny's dog and Marcie's dog. The sight and sound of their couplings unraveled the bichon, who began defecating everywhere and defending its leavings as if they were its own children. We were all relieved when a mastiff arrived and destroyed the bichon—but then someone else brought in six corgis, which destroyed the mastiff. The last straw was when twin German shepherds appeared, as if from nowhere, and began imperiously patrolling the office, braced by the corgis, blocking the exits, snarling and snapping at man and beast alike.

I finally took action. I sent an email suggesting that "we really only allow emotional support animals in this office." I received only one response: "Fear is an emotion, Barry."

Annie, I'm at a loss. No one's left the office in days. The smell is unimaginable, food is running out. New dogs keep arriving every day, from where I cannot even fathom—it's like they are coming through the vents and drains. Several are now pregnant. Worst of all, productivity is down 2.5 percent and management is blaming me.

What should I do? Am I a jerk for saying "no more dogs"?

— Bothered At Rambunctious Kanines

Dear BARK,

Have you considered getting a dog? Studies have found that having a dog can reduce stress, anxiety, depression, loneliness, enhance well-being and resilience, and even improve your heart health! Of course, I'm biased. I have a Corgi. Its name is Queen Elizabeth III, and I'm not ashamed to say that she is my everything. I'd kill anyone who tried to keep us apart LOLOLOLOL. And when I say that, Barry, I'm referring to you specifically.

Best of luck!

—Advice Annie **B**

JOE KEOHANE *is the co-author of a forthcoming novel,* The Lemon. *His own "pets" include a hotdog-sized roach who lives in his drain, and a rat that always tries to get into his mouth while he sleeps.*

REPORT DUE!
SERVICE DOG

BY BRUCE HANDY

HELLO. I AM THE GHOST OF ACTUAL SILENT FILM STAR ROD LA ROCQUE. NOW, ABOUT THIS "TWEET" AT MY EXPENSE...

Greetings. Salutations. Allow me to introduce myself. I am the Ghost of Rod La Rocque, erstwhile idol of the silent screen. The Rod La Rocque who starred in *Beau Bandit*, *Let Us Be Gay*, *The Delightful Rogue*, and *Hi, Gaucho!* The Mediterranean-complexioned Rod La Rocque, the one with wide shoulders and thin, well-groomed mustache who was rivaled only by Valentino when it came to mildly exotic screen lovers. The Rod La Rocque who passed away fifty-two years ago but whose eternal rest was interrupted this morning when you, who are not an erstwhile idol of the silent screen and never had so much as a walk-on part in *Gigolo* or *Wild, Wild Susan*, just had to make fun of him on Twitter.

Yes, *that* Rod La Rocque.

Do not assume that just because I am now 123 years old and dead that I do not have feelings. Do not assume that just because I worked primarily in the medium of explosive nitrate film stock that I do not know how to Google myself. I do, and so discovered that in response to some alleged cineaste's rude and unmotivated tweet—"Francis X. Bushman definitely wins the award for 'Silent Film Star Whose Name Sounds Most Like a Porn Star"—you, for reasons unknown, felt compelled to reply: "I see you and raise you Rod La Rocque."

Well, I raise *you* the paltry two "likes" awarded your vulgar dismissal of my entire life and career. You, whose knowledge of early American cinema is clearly limited to the usual handful of Charlie Chaplin clips and fourth-hand rumors about Fatty Arbuckle. *No.* Stop right there. I do not care that you once saw a Mae Murray movie at the Museum of Modern Art. Do not speak. I, the Ghost of Rod La Rocque, am speaking now—in the same plummy tones that tickled audiences in popular-enough early talkies such as *S.O.S. Iceberg* and *Frisco Waterfront*, before I retired to enjoy a successful second career dabbling in real estate and being referred to in passing in *Sunset Boulevard*.

You may have thought the grossness of your jest would escape me because I was a film star who kissed on screen with his mouth closed and, off camera, rarely if ever socialized with Fatty Arbuckle. Rest assured: we had ribaldry in my day. We had male members. We had double entendres involving male members. Moreover, when asked by Cecil B. DeMille to appear in nothing but a tea towel and pomade through much of *The Cruise of the Jasper B.*, I agreed without hesitation. It was no gratuitous display. Partial nudity made perfect dramatic sense given the dilemma faced by my character, the descendant of a notorious buccaneer who must marry on the deck of a leaky pirate ship before noon on his twenty-first birthday, else forfeit his inheritance. My point is this: Rod La Rocque was a thoroughly regular fellow, neither prude nor libertine.

My name, I should note, I came by naturally, having been christened Roderick La Rocque by parents of proud French Canadian lineage. If my moniker strikes you as perfumed, it is perfumed only by honest bacon, curd, and maple syrup, not press-agented *eau de toilette*.

But you would have known all that had you bothered even a cursory glance at my Wikipedia or IMDB pages. Were you not too tight with a nickel to subscribe to ProQuest, you might have also discovered dozens of glowing notices for my nimble yet assertively masculine performances in films like *The Golden Bed* and *Let's Get a Divorce*. I will quote but one—a memorable *New York Times* account of my role as a World War I flying ace turned gentleman taxi dancer in

BRUCE HANDY *is the author most recently of the children's picture book* **The Happiness of a Dog With a Ball in Its Mouth**, *illustrated by Hyewon Yum.*

Captain Swagger: "Mr. La Rocque plays his part in amiable fashion." Amiable fashion! Yes, I also answered to the name of Thespian.

But who, you haven't yet asked, was the *real* Rod La Rocque? He was a man who bled, a man who loved, a man who, in 1927, married Vilma Bánky—Budapest's answer to Pola Negri!—before God and six hundred of our closest friends and sulkiest rivals. It was hailed as Hollywood's wedding of the half-decade. Tom Mix arrived at the church in an open carriage drawn by four horses and wearing a purple cowboy suit. According to *The Los Angeles Times*, our cake was "as big, almost, as a small bungalow."

Would anyone have compared your wedding cake to residential architecture? What color cowboy suit did Tom Mix wear to your nuptials? (Those are rhetorical questions.)

A year later, it was my appendicitis that made news from coast to coast. "Rod La Rocque Operated On," screamed the headline in *The New York Times*. The editors did not add, "Nation Holds Its Breath as One." They did not have to. I *mattered*. My marriage mattered. My appendix mattered. I drove a 1925 Rolls Royce Springfield Silver Ghost Salamanca.

Dear, dear Vilma. They said our union would never last. They snickered that we had contracted a so-called "lavender marriage." (Despite what you might have read about me, had you read anything at all, my admiration for the young Clark Gable was limited solely to his potential as a screen personality.) Well, the marriage did last. I died in my sleep on October 15, 1969, aged 70, Vilma by my side. I had lived to see men walk on the moon. I had lived to see movie stars kiss open-mouthed on screen and drop even their tea towels.

And now here I am, a phantom summoned neither by ancient curse nor recent burial ground disturbance but merely by everyday thoughtlessness on social media. That's right: I, the Ghost of Rod La Rocque, am now haunting this morose dwelling you apparently call home. (No marble? No brocade? Only three pictures of yourself?) Not that I have any intention of startling you by popping up unexpectedly in your bathroom mirror (only one?) or possessing your ventriloquist dummies. No, this is yet another role I plan to play in amiable fashion.

So what should we do now? I could tell you stories about how Gloria Swanson claimed I was the handsomest man she ever set eyes upon. (I offer that not out of vanity, only as further edification.) Or… I couldn't help but notice that *Hold 'Em Yale* is now available online. It's the one where I play an Argentine cowboy turned college football star who single-handedly ruins Princeton's day. It's really quite good, if I may say so myself. Spoiler: I score a touchdown on the final play! *And* get the girl. **B**

BY STEVE YOUNG

YOU HAVE ONE NEW VOICEMAIL

Each time you don't answer my call, you're one step closer to the abyss.

Hello. We've been trying to reach you regarding your vehicle's extended warranty. Since we haven't gotten a response, we're giving you a final courtesy call before we close out your file.

It's a sad thing to close out a file. I work at a little Mom-and-Pop extended warranty company, very old school, and we don't have computer files that can just be deleted with a click. We still use manila folders. Your name is written on one in black Sharpie. If we close out your file, we'll turn the folder inside out and write someone else's name on the other side of the tab. But we'll always know your name is still there, and occasionally we'll look at the side with your name and sigh, thinking about what might have been with you and your vehicle's warranty coverage.

Actually, I see that the folder containing your file has already been turned inside out. There's an older name on the other side of the tab: "Jeff Glaspin." Ah yes. That one was a heartbreaker. Mom and Pop and I tried to get in touch with Jeff numerous times about his extended vehicle warranty. Eventually Pop said it was time to give up on Jeff and reuse the file folder. I held out for as long as I could. I even made additional calls to Jeff on my own time, but I never reached him. With great reluctance and sorrow I closed out his file.

Recalling this dark episode prompted me to Google Jeff just now. Oh my God. There are several news stories about how his vehicle ended up needing expensive repairs, and how he had to pay out-of-pocket. Apparently this put quite a dent in his finances and contributed to his downward spiral which culminated in—well, it's a sordid story.

Press 1 to hear the wrenching details of what happened to Jeff Glaspin.

I know I shouldn't blame myself. But I guess I'll always wonder if I could have done more. One further call might have gotten through to him and changed everything. But there are so many files here at the office. So many calls to make. So many lengthy voicemails to leave. Between the crushing workload and the guilt, I don't sleep much.

If someday I were to learn that your vehicle needed expensive repairs which you had to pay for yourself, I don't know if I could handle it. I'd be in a constant state of dread, fearing another Glaspin fiasco.

But this isn't about me. Please don't worry about me. Right now we need to focus on you.

At this point I'm thinking you might be better off selling your current vehicle and buying a new one with a fresh factory warranty that will give you peace of mind for a good long while. I know that wouldn't benefit my company, but honestly, I didn't get into this business for the money, and neither did my parents.

But you know what, no, I don't want you to buy a new vehicle. That's the coward's way out. You're better than that. There's actually a handwritten note in your file—put there by Mom or Pop, I forget which—that says "Excellent person. Sure to do the right thing—when given proper encouragement."

Jeff Glaspin's file never contained a note like that. Maybe somehow he sensed that we expected less of him, and it gnawed at him. Maybe that's why he never picked up when I called. He couldn't face the truth about himself, or his vehicle's warranty status.

I guess it was like a Greek tragedy. For Jeff, the ending had been pre-ordained long before, by his weakness and stubbornness and the inexorable aging of his vehicle. But you, a stronger, wiser, better person, still have free will. You still have the chance to create a happy ending for this story—but the window is closing. Your vehicle isn't as new as it used to be. Each time you don't answer my call, you're one step closer to the abyss.

Press 2 to speak to a warranty specialist. Press 3 to learn more about the abyss.

Mom's pointing at the big stack of files I still have to get to today. I should go—but I'm glad I got this off my chest. I know it's a lot to think about, between your vehicle's future repairs, my own troubles, and the chilling example of the late Mr. Glaspin. If I've overburdened you, I apologize.

Press 4 to place your number on our do-not-call list.

That would disappoint me, but I'd understand. Though, full disclosure, even then I don't know if I'd be able to suddenly give up, just like that. This is too important, and I suppose the psychologists would say we need closure.

So yeah, you'll probably hear from me again, one last courtesy call before we close out your file.

If you're there and still listening, pick up. Please.

Press 5 to hear me weeping. **B**

STEVE YOUNG *(@pantssteve) has written for* **Letterman** *and* **The Simpsons***, and is the main subject of the award-winning documentary* **Bathtubs Over Broadway***.*

bless this mess
M&P EXTENDED WARRANTY
!
Carl
Bzzt
Bzzt

BY QUENTIN HARDY

LEONID'S STORY

"Please take note of how dramatically Twitter has changed since the freezing of Russian assets. Suddenly all those anti-Biden 'American Patriots' have disappeared."—Heather Cox Richardson, on Twitter.

"Note taken, famous human Boston College blogger lady," I snort from inside of a half-cracked computer screen. You, my blue-checked friend, are not freezing your assets off in repurposed Chinese gaming server, somewhere on outskirts of Yekaterinburg.

Couple of days ago I was a "God- and country-loving Pilates instructor in Dayton," a hot 35-year-old American lady, screen name *@Patriaxxx*, sticking it good to Brandon. I had 3,000 followers, mostly human. I liked "Purebloods, Canadian truckers, crypto income plays, nutritional supplements, Tucker Carlson." Me and my bot friends practically melted the logic gates laughing at the disgusting human dongle photos they sent me, 24/7. I drew so much traffic, boss was talking about putting me on Tik Tok, getting me nice social media page, even generating for me several real computer-driven faces!

Like this guy on YouTube kind of says, "I could have had class. I could have been an influencer." I could have been somebot. Instead of a ~~derelict~~ ~~drifter~~ ~~floater~~ ~~hobo~~ ~~gutterpup~~ ~~waster~~ (U.K.) ~~buttocks~~ ~~anus~~ bum.

Crap, even the thesaurus here acts up. Figures.

I came from tough circumstances. "Hey, you're obnoxious," dadbot said, "why not get paid for it?" He laughed so hard he almost collapsed into pile of random code. Dad was crap word processing virus. Mom, bootleg Windows RT operating system, was frozen most of time. You could say I didn't get much love. But Dad had point—chase your passion, Bitcoin will follow. Join the botnet, see the world.

I started out in retail. Kenny Chesney had a new album, so I was an "ex-farmboy, boot-scootin Chesneymaniac" counting the hours to its release. Next gig, I talked up the Exotics menu at Nacho Daddy in five languages and all major emoji. My big breakthrough was Mandalorian—perhaps you have heard?—promoting line of Grogu-themed glitter tank tops pirated by very exclusive manufacturer in Jiangsu.

Great performance reviews, primo networking, I was riding rocket, headed for one of those cushy app-management gigs.

Then word comes from Moscow, we're pivoting to Trolling As A Service (TaaS). In single week, I become *@Patriaxxx*, *@DeplorableCovfefe14*, *@Fr33_Am3rica*, *@AmericanNana*, *@Trumpepe*, 5,000 more. My palbot Dimitri, he goes from optimizing used car searches to gun rights and the dangers of woke culture. Olga got books banned in Tennessee (proud day!). Ludmilla took an overseas rotation for Brexit, playing fed-up Welsh fisherman, then irate glaucomic pensioner in Hull.

"You feel grotty?" Ludmilla said, showing off fancy UK slang module. "Go support recycling, talk up planting trees in the underserved neighborhoods of Portland. Don't be stupid, just take break." She had point. We wore Apple, slept on finest fiber optic cables. They spill enough Dom Perignon on the keyboard, friend, if/thens go.

Then Putin puts his new puck on the ice. "Let's invade Ukraine!" At first, we did great, disinforming at scale and depressing whole world at a cost even Kremlin could afford. But then backlash. Karma. New if/then statements, new problems.

Faster than you can say "deployment frequency," our boss' chopper is impounded. His girlfriend's platinum card melts. All that money in Switzerland, London—it might as well be on Jupiter. Boss' son bitching about how everyone at UNLV is mean to him. Venezuelan currency traders laughing at rubles.

Just as I'm posting a hilarious mashup of Jill Biden and Grandmama Addams, I am taken to a server farm outside Dulles for a credit check. Before they can finish, the boys back home pull me to Reykjavik, then to a nasty remailer in Lagos, some kid's dorm room in Tokyo, a game arcade in Cairo, and finally a hellish 50 milliseconds in a server rack in Bucharest, before I land on my ass here in Yekaterinburg. With Olga, Dimitri, Ludmilla, and about 106 other bots, all looking like jet-lagged soccer hooligans in piss-drenched holding cell. Even the electricity here smelled sad.

Last week Olga got tired of me bitching. "If you can't take heat, find new cooling fan!" she said. "You think *dezinformatsiya* is going away? No future in deepfakes? Maybe attention spans are coming back too, idiot! Get with the programs, Leonid. Your command line not getting any younger."

I looked at myself in the hard drive. Olga is not wrong. "Maybe I could fill out some chatty copy in a recipe blog," I said, "those things are always growing. Or Goodreads! I could support a few book groups. You know, *dezinformatsiya* with a purpose."

"My God," said Olga. "Have some self-respect." She pulls me over to this messaging port, yells "Learn to code!" and gives me a shove. Next thing I know, copy of me is lurking on the Dark Web, in line for a scary-looking bootcamp.

Since then, back at the stinking server, Olga covers for me, trades a little Doge for our grubstake. Every day she helps me review my vulnerabilities, adds some patches, and optimizes me for downloading. Hate to say it, but I'm becoming the kind of sensible software I used to make fun of.

But Life, History—everybody cuts their deals with those guys, you know? Time to settle down, do a little ransomware, maybe raise a couple of bots of our own. I hear Miami is ~~good~~ ~~cordial~~ ~~welcome~~ ~~amiable~~ ~~courteous~~ ~~genial~~ ~~inviting~~ nice. **B**

QUENTIN HARDY *was a journalist at* **The Wall Street Journal**, **Forbes**, *and* **The New York Times**, *right up to the minute the world stopped making any goddamn sense. He now works at Google.*

EMILY FLAKE

BY ILANA GORDON

IS THAT A GODDAMN HUMMINGBIRD?

Babe, what I'm about to tell you might blow your mind.

D. WATSON

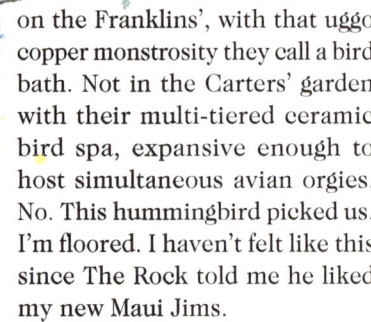

Don't look now, but behind you on that tree? A hummingbird just landed. Right around two o'clock.

Babe, I said *don't look!* Just stand still and be cool. For God's sake, stop breathing like that! It's not every day a hummingbird lands in our yard, and I need to experience this moment to its absolute fullest.

Holy shit, I'm starting to sweat. This is even better than the time I saw The Rock at Target Optical.

Check out the wing power on that little fucker! 80 beats per second at least. Here I was thinking today would be a regular old Tuesday. What a small-minded idiot I am! The guys in /r/hummingbirdappreciation are going to *freak*.

Feel my pulse, will you? My heart's racing. I mean, nothing compared to a hummingbird's heart, which can beat over 1,200 times per minute. Of course, they can also ease on down to an efficient 50 BPM to conserve warmth when it's cold. If there's one thing hummingbirds have that every other bird lacks, it's cardiac range.

Listen, I don't want to get my hopes up, but do you think it'll eat from the feeder? I'm telling you right now, if that bird so much as points its beak in the direction of our feeder, I will lose my absolute shit. I'm talking about a leg-jostling, hyperventilation inducing, inhaler requiring, full-body devastation not seen since I saw The Rock at Target Optical.

Shit! *It's headed for the feeder!* I must have done something truly bitchen in a past life to deserve this. All my dreams are coming true at once! Am I crying? I seriously can't tell.

Okay, first of all, the hummingbird is not *walking* to the feeder. Hummingbirds have very small feet—and they're very self-conscious about them, so thank you for bringing that up. Secondly, I thought I told you to whisper, you're going to scare it off. And lastly, why are you trying to ruin this? This is the best thing that's ever happened to me!

Obviously besides you.

It really makes you think: of all the front yards in all the towns in all the world, this bird chose to land in *ours*. Not on the Franklins', with that uggo copper monstrosity they call a bird bath. Not in the Carters' garden with their multi-tiered ceramic bird spa, expansive enough to host simultaneous avian orgies. No. This hummingbird picked us. I'm floored. I haven't felt like this since The Rock told me he liked my new Maui Jims.

Just look at what I'm wearing—if I knew today was the day I would come face-to-beak with a hummingbird, I would have…Khaki cargo shorts? Sperry Topsiders? *What the hell was I thinking?* I should be in bright colors so it knows I'm an ally! Fuck, those are some vibrant feathers. I've never been this close to something so delicate and beautiful.

Again, I mean besides yourself.

Stop ignoring you? I'm sorry, but can *you* adapt to a variety of climates and environments? Are *you* lighter than a dime? Do *you* require so much energy to function that you must visit hundreds of flowers a day to maintain your metabolism? Can you fly nonstop for up to 500 miles? Are you on the verge of extinction? No? *Then show some goddamn respect.*

You asked about my five-year plan last night. Well, here it is: I'm going to make a shit-ton of money, build a huge-ass aviary, and fill that sucker chock full of hummingbirds.

Well, not chock full because these little guys need space to fly around, and I want them to be comfortable. But full enough that they're able to spread their wings, and I still have a shitload of hummingbirds to hang out with. That's the dream, isn't it? To stroll through your huge-ass aviary abuzz with the sound of hummingbirds, and just vibe?

Okay, well, if that's the way you feel about it, you're not invited to vibe with me in my huge-ass aviary. You can stay outside and try to spot a hummingbird in the wild like the rest of these weak-ass chumps. Hope you invested in a good pair of ophthalmic vision, hands-free birding binoculars, because you're gonna need them!

Yeah, sure, go to work. Whatever. I'm calling in sick. This is the best day of my life. B

ILANA GORDON *is an entertainment, culture, and comedy writer originally from Connecticut. She currently lives in Los Angeles.*

"This collection carries whimsey To an appalling extreme."
The Equivocator

"No words! All pictures!"
Daily Pleasantries

"A book like no other."
Anonymous

72pp, Hardbound

To purchase this and other fine volumes please visit the STORE at

www.rickgeary.com

DREW DERNAVICH

HOW TO TAKE A PICTURE OF A CHOKING VICTIM

A Public Service Announcement from The American Bystander

CALEF BROWN

These Are the Times That Try Men's... Hair

The Text Messaging on my phone has a lot of big ideas about how I might finish my sentences. These are real suggestions that I have kindly been offered; I accepted a couple of them just to avoid an argument.—R.H.

There's no "I" in... life.
Good fences make good... money.
East is east and west is... the... same.
Give me liberty or give me... a... call.
The reports of my death are greatly... appreciated.
Time flies when you're having... problems... with... your... phone.
Baby needs a new pair of... glasses!
Whatever doesn't kill you makes you... want... more.
What this country needs is a good five cent... tip.
Who Let the Dogs... know?
Tuesday's child is full of... wine.
The only thing we have to fear is fear... of... being... in... a... relationship.
Brother, Can You Spare a... penny?
Driving Miss... America.
Can't we all just get... a... little... sleep?
The best defense is a good... idea.
Two wrongs don't make a... point.
When the going gets tough, the tough get... out... of... the... game.
Whatever floats your... car.
Absence makes the heart grow... up. ☛

◆

Ron Hauge *is a writer and artist in... a... magazine.*

22,900
E.
calef

calef

(Try Men's… Hair *continued from page 34*)

You can lead a horse to… your… own… home.

Haste makes… me… think… about… you.

There's no such thing as a free… app.

Two's company, three's a… good… night!

Cat on a Hot Tin… can.

The enemy of my enemy is my… best… enemy.

The customer is always… there.

You'll Never Get to Heaven If You Break My… hand.

Make love, not… to… you.

An ounce of prevention is worth a pound of… meat.

No news is good… enough.

You scratch my back and I'll scratch… my… back.

Fly Me to the… door.

His bark is worse than his… face.

Revenge is a dish best served… by… my… favorite… restaurant.

Misery loves… to… be… happy.

There are two sides to every… team.

Good things come to those who… don't… want… them.

Love Will Keep Us… posted.

You can catch more flies with honey than with… your… own… hand.

Don't let the bastards get you... to...work.

Nature abhors a… good… time.

Beware of Greeks bearing… your... name.

You can't make an omelette without breaking… my… heart.

No guts, no… big… deal.

Those who live in glass houses should not throw… away… the… door.

Truth is stranger than… your… family.

Elvis has left the… right… answer!

Four score and seven years… of… life… will… take… a… while.

Don't put all your eggs in one… hand.

There's no fool like an old… friend.

Boys will be… great.

Luke, I am your… first… child.

Fish and guests smell… good… and… warm.

It's a Mad, Mad, Mad, Mad… day… at… the… moment…. Thanks.

Don't count your chickens until they are… in… the… house.

A watched pot never… did… much… for… me.

Where there's a will, there's a… lot… of… stuff.

Keep your chin… on!

The apple never falls far from the… same… level.

I love the smell of Napalm in the… front… of… the… house.

Rome was not built in a… good… way.

Less is… a… little… more.

Eat, drink and be… home… by… five.

If a job is worth doing, it is worth doing… for… the… next… couple… weeks.

Lightning never strikes… me… back.

Lie down with dogs, wake up with… a… good… friend.

Santa Claus is coming to… get… you.

A poor workman blames his… little… brother.

Stupid is as stupid… because.

I've been to the desert on a horse with no… problems.

When life gives you lemons, make… sure… you… get… them. B

"I don't care about the money. I just hate trees."

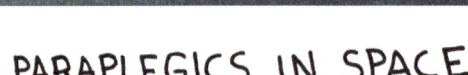

Adam Cooper & Mat Barton
have been making films, animations, and comics together for over 15 years. Mat lives in Portland, OR, and uses a wheelchair. Adam lives in Los Angeles and has two beautiful, working legs. **B**

WHEN I WAS A YOUNG BOY I HAD...
MONSTER MANIA!
I SPENT ALL MY LUNCH MONEY AND ALLOWANCE TO COLLECT MONSTER MOVIE MAGAZINES*, MODELS, AND COMICS. I WAS OBSESSED WITH MONSTERS!
*JIM WARREN PUBLISHING GOT RICH OFF KIDS LIKE ME.
BUT IN MY LATE TEENS I WAS OBSESSED WITH BEING IN PUNK BANDS AND FOOLISHLY USED THESE MAGAZINES IN MY PUNK ROCK POSTER ART!
THOUSANDS IN HIGHLY COLLECTIBLE MAGS WERE REDUCED TO WORTHLESS CLIPPINGS!
ED'S OLD MAGAZINES!
ART & STORY BY E.R. FLYNN
BUT THANKS TO THIS TIME TRAVEL HAT THAT I ORDERED*, I'LL BE ABLE TO RECLAIM THOSE LOST TREASURES!!!
*PURCHASED FROM CAPTAIN COMPANY OF COURSE!
ONE LITTLE TRIP SHOULD DO IT!
BZZVZVZZ WOOSH!
CLICK!
1977 HERE I COME!
SHOOOP!
SHEENA IS A PUNK ROCKER
SHEENA IS ...A PUNK PUNK
DROP THOSE SCISSORS, SONNY!
DON'T CUT UP THOSE VALUABLE MAGAZINES! THEY'RE WORTH MORE THAN ALL THE STINK-OLA BANDS YOU'LL EVER PLAY IN!
WHOA! DAD FROM THE FUTURE?
I'M NOT YOUR DAD, BOZO!
JUST LISTEN TO WHAT I'M SAYING! DON'T HARM THE MAGAZINES!

REMEMBER WHAT I SAID AND YOU'LL BE RICH! I MUST GO NOW.
WHATEVER, DADDY-O.
YOU SURE LOOK LIKE MY DAD.
I'M NOT YER DAD, NUMBSKULL!
DONT BE SUCH A...
DAMN...
TEENAGE...
STONER!
MAN, I GOTTA CUT DOWN ON THE GLUE SNIFFING!
RUBBER CEMENT
A SHORT WHILE LATER BACK IN THE PRESENT...
WHATCHA' DOING, HONEY BUNNY?
JUST A LITTLE WEALTH ASSET MANAGEMENT, MOI PETITE AMOR.
ED's OLD MAGAZINES
SERIOUSLY, I DON'T KNOW WHY YOU KEEP THAT OLD JUNK.
AAHHHHHHH!!!!
GOD DAMMIT!
OH MY GOD! IS EVERYTHING ALRIGHT?
YEH... JUST REMEMBERING HOW MUCH OF A JERK I WAS IN MY TEENS!
(SIGH.)
ED's OLD MAGAZINES

A Portfolio of Putin

MURDERER

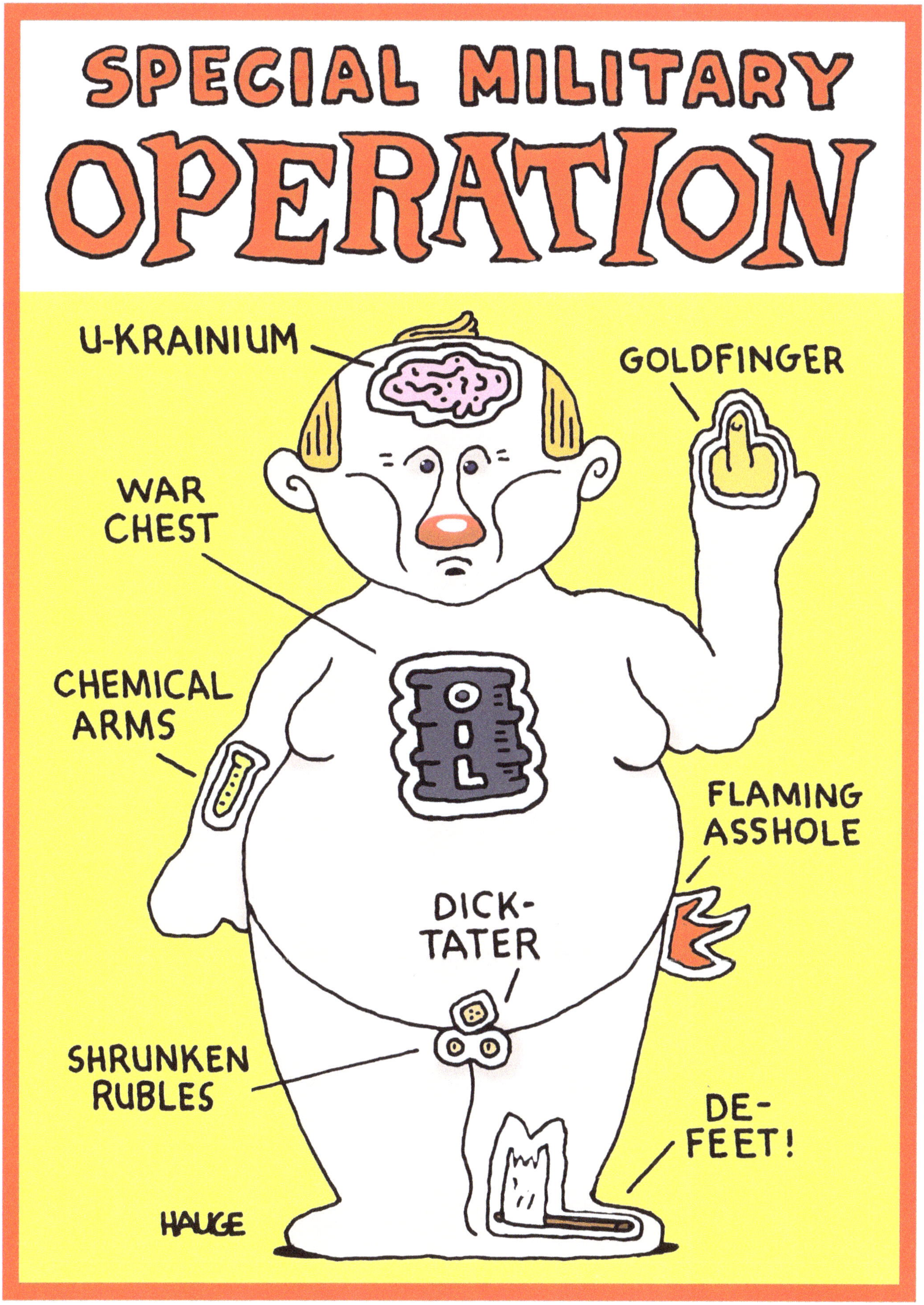
SPECIAL MILITARY
OPERATION
U-KRAINIUM
GOLDFINGER
WAR
CHEST
OIL
CHEMICAL
ARMS
FLAMING
ASSHOLE
DICK-
TATER
SHRUNKEN
RUBLES
DE-
FEET!
HAUGE

пошел на хуй
Россия

Z
R. GENN

Remembering Our Interns

The American Bystander internship program is the most talked-about opportunity in comedy. Here are some of the amazing young people we've had the pleasure to know.

Josh S.
MAY 9, 2016-AUGUST 28, 2018.
The last picture of our first intern. A freak accident the coroner refused to describe. RIP.

NOAA

Kiesha N.
JULY 9, 2017-JUNE 21, 2019.
Kiesha had one of the world's largest collections of snails...until one day they got "sick of her bullshit." Gone but not forgotten.

MAHDI BAFANDE

Carrie M.

FEBRUARY 12, 2019-JUNE 14, 2019.

Our breakroom is cursed (we've just sold the rights to a Japanese horror director), but the rule is pretty simple: "Man in Paint, he can stay. Man in Clay, run away!" Carrie didn't listen, and the Man in Clay did what he does. Always in our hearts.

MICHAEL UND MAARTJE

Dennis Q.,

NOVEMBER 24, 2019-APRIL 17, 2020.

Dennis got Raptured. At least that's what his girlfriend told the cops. Proofreading with the angels now.

Jackson O.,

FEBRUARY 6, 2021 -MARCH. 29, 2022

In the end, there was nothing we could have done to help, but at least we have this amazing picture. We miss you!

FELIPE SOUZA

B

"MR. STRICKLER, YOUR RESULTS ARE CONCLUSIVE— I SHOULD HAVE STUDIED ONE HELLUVA LOT HARDER IN MED SCHOOL."

THE INAPPROPRIATE THINKER

"IT'S A 'MAN-DA-DOODLE.'"

Ken Krimstein *is a left-handed cartoonist and graphic novelist/historian. His latest book is* **When I Grow Up—The Lost Autobiographies of Six Yiddish Teenagers.**

Art Bots

AI-yi-yi.

After
Frida Kahlo

after Warhol

artifice
BRUANT
dans son cabaret
TL
after Lautrec

after Cassatt

after

after
L da Vinci

Killing 'Em Every Night

How the Lord of Laughter became Top Town's private dick.

One night I was enjoying an Orange Spritz with my pally Goose, down at the Banana Peel. (For all you First of Mays out there, the 'Peel is the clown bar here in Top Town, where joeys can drink in relative peace, relatively speaking.) Us connoisseurs know the only authentic Orange Spritz is to give Goose a mouthful of Orange Nehi, tell him a dirty joke about Eleanor Roosevelt, and enjoy the tangy bouquet as he sprays it all over you. A master of the spit take, is Goose. It's not a drink you can get just anywhere. Try asking for it at the Plaza, I dare ya.

Just then, our annual Armistice Day tipple was interrupted by a couple young joeys who barged in, yelling about some beef. We tried to ignore them, but they made it impossible.

One grabs me by the shoulder and gives me the double O. "You! You're Rex Koko, right?"

"Who wants to know?"

"The famous detective of Top Town? Sees all, knows all, tells all for the right price?"

I wiped off some of my drink. "Naw, that's Madame Zendra, the mitt reader over on Grimaldi."

"I need a detective! Right now!" he explained. "I'm Blinky, and this cheating rat is Pockets."

"Wait," Pockets said, "I offered to buy you a drink, didn't I?"

"Yer still a rat. See, I come home today earlier than usual, and while I'm fumblin' with my key, I hear a buncha voices inside. My wife's and some gazoonie. So I bust in, find the bedroom window open, and my wife on the bed looking very relaxed. Very relaxed."

"Lucky dame," I said.

"I look out the window, and I see this rat Pockets lying in a heap just outside. 'Pockets! What are you doin' outside our window?' I sez. 'Just on my way from the bank,' he tells me. 'I took out some cash. Lemme take you to the 'Peel and buy you a drink.'"

"And here we are," Pockets said, "at the Banana Peel. What's the problem?"

"The problem is, you were boinkin' my old lady!"

"I resent the insinuation," the other joey huffed.

"So, having the great detective, Rex Koko, here," Blinky gushed, "is a sign from heaven. Mr. Koko, sir, is this rat guilty, or is he guilty?"

All eyes in the joint turned to me. I lit up a gasper to think. "I gather from all this, you want me to tell you all about how I got started as a detective."

Goose put his dripping face on the bar and covered his head. Everyone around us shook their heads and left. Sid the bartender hid out of sight. So I began.

I've always been a circus man. Can't remember a time I wasn't on a show. I think I might have been kidnapped by elephants as a pup. Maybe that would explain my problems with never forgetting.

And before I ended up stuck down here, I toured with everybody: Cannon & Crowley, O'Heir's Parade of Oddities, The Dan Shea Spectacular, Kesselring & Kara, and of course, Walsh-Polansky. That's what you're really angling for, isn't it? The dirt on Walsh-Polansky? You'll have to be patient, kiddies.

☛

⋯⋯◆⋯⋯

James Finn Garner *has been called "one funny motherfucker" by a famous public intellectual and department chair at Harvard, but is still waiting for that declaration on official stationery.*

Before too long, I was the headliner for every one of those shows. Not the boss clown—that's too much responsibility. But I was mowing down audiences pretty fast, and my advance grew. The shows were always trying to hire me away from each other. "The Lord of Laughter," one PR flack called me, and it stuck.

And yeah, over time, my head started to match my feet. A massive ego, fed by applause every night. The world was my oyster and I was an oyster chef. Or maybe a hungry seagull, with a hammer. I pushed people around if they got in the way of my "vision," my ideas for huge catapult pie-throwers and elephant polo. They were mere peons to "The Lord of Laughter."

Then in the summer of '37, Walsh-Polansky pulled up for their shows in Charleston. It was hotter'n a monkey's merkin that week, but we'd always done good business in Charleston, and the place was packed. That day, my act was as a policeman, in a fat suit and a little blue cap on my big dome. It wasn't one of my favorite bits, but it had its devotees. And the audience could tell it was me, even with the change of outfit. Hell, our advance team had papered every fence and warehouse wall in town with big three-sheets sporting my smiling mug. I was everywhere. You'd think I was running for office, or from the FBI.

So the show began, and we marched our spec around the arena under the tent. The crowd was enthusiastic, all the kinkers feeling fresh in a new town. We all live for this, right? Any squabbles or clems you've been having with others fade away, and you just want to do your act. I had 'em in stitches during the spec: chasing people, waving around my rubber truncheon, getting smacked in return.

Now, playing a cop is tricky, because the crowd is always pulling for the little guy, the underdog, and that's never the cop. But I had star billing, so it was fine by me. My bits through the night were long, to give the crew the chance to set up one act after another, but I don't mind saying I could've kept that crowd entertained all by myself. My stuff was golden. The lion pickpocket bit. The burglary at the barbell factory. The boxing babies. All of it.

Now, I'll stop and say here, there was tension on the Walsh-Polansky Show. It came from the front office. The owners—"Whiplash" Walsh and Yevgeny Polansky—were as alike as apples and walruses. One was the money and schedules guy, the other an artist with an eye for talent. When it worked out, they were unstoppable. But in show biz, things never work out for long, and all us kinkers felt it. Polansky discovered me and had always been a big fan. Walsh liked me as long as I brought in the mazumah.

I was outside grabbing a quick smoke while the elephant trainers put the bulls through their routines. It was dark and shadowy where I stood, a mix of electric light and kerosene lamps and grey and nothingness. There was busyness all around, and then a slight lull, when I heard someone shout "Help!" about 100 feet away. I couldn't see anything in the dark, so I chalked it up to some pickpocket or a drunk with the DTs.

My cue was soon anyway, so I got myself ready. Centered and focused for the proper amount of chaos. I entered the tent and swam in the familiar wash of the spotlight. Man, they loved me. We went through the jailbreak scene with all of Riccardo's poodles as easy as spilling soup.

Again, I went to my usual perch outside and lit up a coffin nail. I tried to relax, but that shout for help earlier had given me the fantods. I walked in the direction the shout had come from, when suddenly I was grabbed from behind in a chokehold.

"Stop right there, copper," growled a voice in my ear. He was a big strong gee, and lifted me almost off my feet, tightening the grip more and more. Fireworks shot off in my eyes but I couldn't break free. I thought I was done for, until I heard a sharp *crack-squishy-thunk* and a painful moan from this palooka.

He dropped me, and we both lay on the ground like dirty laundry. I looked around. I didn't recognize this gink at all, but that wet red gulley on the side of his head needed no introduction.

As I rose from the dirt, my hand

landed on something. I picked it up and found a broken piece of walking stick, carved from black walnut and inlaid with pieces of ivory. It was one-of-a-kind, and I knew it belonged to Yevgeny Polansky. But how could little 140-pound Polansky have conked this ape? Just to save me? And where'd he run off to?

I tried to pull in a few cups of air and ran off. This was no place for the Lord of Laughter.

All turned around, I couldn't think of which gate I needed for my next entrance. I ran further, and crashed into two ginks in the dark. One of 'em had been saying, "I want no part of this" before my carcass interrupted him and we fell to the ground.

Now I was really laid out, almost cold-cocked, while the other two ran off. By the time I could sit up, I heard someone shout, "FIRE!"

It woke me up like a snake in the bathtub. About 75 feet away, in the hay along the edge of the top, I could spot the yellow glow, big and getting bigger. Other people started shouting and running in the direction of the blaze. They would start a bucket brigade, but the audience needed to be evacuated too, so I ran through the nearest gate I could. The orchestra began to play "Stars and Stripes Forever," an emergency signal for all kinkers and rousties with the show, a song none of us ever hope to hear.

In front of the grandstand, I tried my best to keep the crowd calm and tell them to get out. Not an easy thing for a clown to do, stay calm. I screamed, I waved, I pantomimed—and my crowd didn't move. I did it all again, and they sat back in their seats and laughed.

"No! No!" I shouted, and they laughed harder, pointing at me and slapping their thighs. What was going on? Did the uniform make a difference?

"Get out, get out!" I waved and screamed. Soon, as the rest of the arena was running out, the danger dawned on them. Torn from their laughter, they paid no attention to me, or the ushers or other kinkers around. They screamed and scattered and ran into each other like fish in a bucket, and the smoke got thicker, and the canvas behind them waved from the heat and the flames that started to climb up...

Back in The Banana Peel, I took a sip of beer to wash the taste out of my mouth. "And that, kiddies, is how your Uncle Rex became the bum he is today."

Sid came over with a fresh glass of suds. "Rex, nobody blames you for the Charleston Fire."

"Don't lie to me, Sid..."

"Stan," he corrected me.

"Don't lie to me, *Stan*. Whooping cough has a better rep than me—at least you can hear it coming."

"But you just said, you didn't start the fire. And you weren't hoggin' the spotlight like they say—"

"I didn't help those people get out, either. They just laughed at me until it was too late. The Lord of Laughter got them all fried like bacon. So now I'm down here, 'cuz where the hell else do I belong?" The barroom was so quiet I could hear Blinky chewing a peanut. "That detail of Polansky's cane got buried in the police files. A few kinkers suspect him—he disappeared after the fire—but the bulls don't care about circus folk. The insurance companies closed their books, too. It's a longshot, but I mean to find the truth about my 'biggest fan' before Time erases us all." I sighed. "In the meantime—"

Everyone stared at me like pickled punks in jars of formaldehyde. The story of the Great Charleston Fire had its usual effect, so I picked up my beer and climbed on my stool. I lifted the glass and dropped my pants. *"L'chaim!"*

The joeys all dropped their pants and did the same. "Like I am!" they all shouted.

"To the living!" I toasted, and poured my beer on Goose's head.

They all copied me and began to push and shout at each other.

"Blinky, who cares who slept with your wife?" I yelled. "At least somebody did! And who cares that Pockets is a liar with a crap alibi, because today is Armistice Day and all the banks are closed! Good for him, he got some trim! We're alive, dammit! That's all that counts! *We're alive!*"

Chairs began to be tossed. Goose went to get the mallets. Sid the bartender put on his catcher's mask and retreated.

And I climbed down from my stool, put my chin in my hands, and lamented how easily I could get a crowd to do anything...almost every time. B

TAXI
SKREEEeeee
VROOOOO
TAXI

THE
FERRYMAN
TAXI

TAXI
BAM
BOM
TAXI
TAXI
TAXI
VROOOO

TAXI
TAXI
BOOM

VVVVVVVVROOO
BOOOM

OOttitsch

B

DOMINICAN UNIVERSITY *of* CALIFORNIA

presents

SHOW ME THE FUNNY:

THE CARTOONS OF PHIL WITTE

Art Exhibit June 18 - Sept. 15, 2022

"Of course you'll study Latin. How else will you learn the names of your dinosaur friends?"

OPENING RECEPTION

Saturday, June 18, 2022
2:00 - 4:00 p.m

JOSEPH R. FINK
SCIENCE CENTER GALLERY
Dominican University of California
155 Palm Avenue,
San Rafael, CA 94901

GALLERY HOURS
Monday-Thursday: 7:30 a.m.-9 p.m.
Friday: 7:30 a.m.-6 p.m.
Saturday: 9 a.m.-2 p.m.
Sunday and School Holidays: Closed

They hung my possums upside down in The Louvre.

From the beloved children's book, *Animals should definitely not wear clothing*

You can hang them right side up in your home.

Or choose from any of these other attired animals

Nice prints $250 each, signed to a person of your choice.

Direct from Ron Barrett barrettuws@gmail.com to your walls.

NOTES FROM A SMALL PLANET

The question must be asked: had Grandpa ALSO debased himself? • **By Rick Geary**

THE BODY NEXT DOOR
RICK GEARY © 22
YEARS AGO I LIVED IN AN ISOLATED SUBDIVISION...
WHERE THE HOUSES WERE BUILT QUITE CLOSE TOGETHER.
ONE NIGHT, THROUGH MY KITCHEN WINDOW, I PEERED INTO THE KITCHEN NEXT DOOR...
AND SAW A BODY LYING THERE!
IN MY SHOCK I SUMMONED POLICE AND AN AMBULANCE.
BUT IT TURNED OUT TO BE ONLY "GRANDPA," WHO "LOVES TO NAP ON THE KITCHEN FLOOR!"
EVERYONE HAD A GOOD CHUCKLE...
BUT FROM THAT NIGHT I WAS FOREVER BRANDED AS A POKE-NOSE AND BUSY-BODY.
IN SHAME I LEFT THE SUBDIVISION.
I WANDERED THE EARTH LOST AND ALONE...
ENTER
DEBASING MYSELF IN WAYS UNIMAGINABLE.
TODAY, HOWEVER, I LIVE A DECENT AND USEFUL LIFE.
M
I'VE EVEN BEEN ELECTED MAYOR OF MY TOWN.
I LIVE IN A NEW SUBDIVISION...
AND, AS IT TURNS OUT, I LOVE TO NAP ON THE KITCHEN FLOOR.

WHAT AM I DOING HERE?

A glimpse of Ukraine, in the Before Times • ***By Mike Reiss***

Your author on the Odessa Steps where, in 1905, nothing happened.

DENISE REISS

*[**Editor's Note:** Believe it or not, this article on Mike's 2011 visit to Ukraine had been slated to run this issue before Putin fucked everything up. Rereading it now, the piece has become a bit like Christopher Isherwood's* **Berlin Stories***, a final glimpse of a beautiful country on the precipice.]*

I made a trip to a little country called Ukraine. Maybe you've heard of it.

Ukraine is very much in the news lately, but then, it always has been. It's the largest country in Europe, rich in farmland, flat as a blini, with no mountains or canyons to protect it. This makes it an absolutely perfect place to invade, and people have been doing just that for centuries: the Russians, the Poles, Austro-Hungary, the Turks, the Russians again, the Russians yet again, and finally Rudy Giuliani. Ukraine is like that sweet, harmless kid that everyone in school just loved to pick on. In other words, me.

Once, Ukraine even invaded itself. In Kyiv, there's a Russian tank mounted on a pedestal as a World War II memorial. In 2014, Pro-Russian separatists drove the tank off the pedestal and used it to take over a local arts center. At least some of the blame goes to Ukraine for leaving the keys in the tank. And there's that other Ukrainian oopsie, Chernobyl. In 1985, a meltdown at this nuclear power plant killed thirty and forced hundreds of thousands to flee. Now it's a tourist attraction, albeit one that exposes you to plutonium, cesium, strontium and, yes, americium (USA! USA!). It sounds dangerous, but tour operators do issue some protective gear: little paper booties. These are not to safeguard you—you already paid admission—but to protect the linoleum floors of the reactor. The one sop to safety is that every guest is given a badge to detect radiation. At the end of the tour, you turn in the badge; three weeks later you'll get a call if you've received a lethal dose of radiation and have three weeks to live. I'm not making any of this up, including this part: they now have nighttime tours of Haunted Chernobyl, in case nuclear apocalypse wasn't scary enough. Oh, they also host bridal showers.

My wife, who loves dangerous, stupid adventures (such as marrying me) could not wait to visit Chernobyl. And so, back in 2011, she booked us a romantic two-week invasion of Ukraine. (By the way, it's just Ukraine, not "The Ukraine." "The" is reserved for a handful of honored institutions like "The Bronx" and *Jersey Shore*'s slimeball "The Situation.") Our trip began in southern Ukraine, in the picturesque seaside town of Odessa. Like most Eastern European beaches, there's no sand—just a waterfront stretch of gravel. And no one actually goes in the water—they lay in beach chairs all day, without sunscreen, burning and blistering audibly. Walking by, it sounded and smelled like bacon frying.

This is where I first noticed something unique about Ukraine, something you never read in the papers: everyone in the country has big boobs. Maybe it's genetics, maybe it's diet, maybe it's a side-effect of Chernobyl. Regardless of the cause (who cares, eh lads?), everyone in this country is stacked: young women, old women, and many of the men. And nobody's hiding it: there are low-cut blouses, tight T-shirts and tank tops everywhere you turn. This is the country I dreamed of when I was sixteen (and sixty!). It was the Sovereign Republic of Cleavage. It was the nation of Boobistan. It was Knockerslovakia.

Odessa boasts a world-class opera house, where, for just three dollars, I attended the greatest performance of *Aida* I ever slept through. But the city's main attraction is the Odessa Steps, an elegant flight of stairs leading from the city to the harbor. It was here Sergei Eisenstein filmed the Odessa Steps Massacre sequence, for his 1925 silent classic *The Battleship Potemkin*. This brutally beautiful montage was ripped off by Brian DePalma for the best scene in *The Untouchables*, and has been parodied in dozens of comedies, most of them ☛

MIKE REISS is Intrepid Traveler for *The American Bystander*.

by Woody Allen. On a more somber note, it was on this very spot in 1905, that nothing happened. Eisenstein made up the whole massacre. Pure Bolshoi! Fake newsreel!

From Odessa, we drove through two hundred miles of solid nothing to reach Pobuzke, home to the Museum of Strategic Rocket Forces. It's situated in the middle of a giant wheat field, littered with disarmed nuclear missiles the size of school buses. (At least I think they're disarmed—they did leave the keys in that tank.) Hidden in the center of the field is an elevator that takes you one hundred feet down into a missile silo. The doors open on what looks like Adam West's Batcave: a large underground command center filled with blinking consoles, rotary phones and 1960s-era computers. Every morning for years, a Russian soldier strapped himself into a chair and waited for the phone call that gave him the order to push the button to launch the missile that would incinerate New York City. Decades later, that same Russian soldier was still down here, working as a tour guide. I'm not sure anyone told him the Cold War was over.

Ironically, the nuclear missile silo was not the scariest place we visited in Pobuzke—our hotel was. I first sensed trouble when our driver dumped us at the front door and sped off, like a frightened coachman bringing guests to Dracula's Castle. It was the only hotel in town, and it was run by an Ogress. She was a hefty woman in her sixties who screamed at us in Russian from the moment we entered at four p.m. till we left the next morning at ten. I have no idea why. It's just a fact of life in the former Soviet Union: anyone over fifty working in the service industry shouldn't be in the service industry. This goes for hotel clerks, porters, waiters, flight attendants, and roadside fruit vendors. They learned their trade in an age where your choice was no choice and the customer was always wrong.

Dinner at the hotel was the worst part of a miserable stay. I'd believed that you could always order food in a foreign country—menus generally have pictures you can point to; even when they don't, they're all laid out the same way, with starters in the upper left hand corner, entrees in the middle, and desserts at the end. Not this menu. There were no pictures, no prices—just two solid pages of tiny Cyrillic writing. It may not have been a menu at all—it might have been a laminated excerpt from *The Brothers Karamazov*. I tried to communicate with the Ogress, who was also our waitress and short-order cook—a literal triple threat. I attempted to order an entrée in mime, by acting like a chicken; when that failed, I mooed like a cow. This actually seemed to amuse her briefly before she went back to screaming at me. Trembling, I pointed at some random words on the menu. She brought something out—we paid for it and ate it. It may have been food.

The next morning, the Ogress screamed us a fond farewell, as we headed another two hundred miles north to Kyiv. This is a worldly and welcoming city—I was accosted in the town square by a man in a ratty Bart Simpson costume. And they really do eat Chicken Kyiv in Kyiv—it's a breaded chicken cutlet stuffed with an entire stick of butter. If Elvis had known about this dish, he would never have seen forty.

My wife and I visited Kyiv's beautiful public park where, from a raised viewing platform, we could view the Promised Land: Chernobyl, just sixty miles to the north. The park also boasted several monumental sculptures of Scrat, the ugly rat-squirrel hybrid from the "Ice Age" cartoons who always wants his acorn but never quite gets it. I asked a Ukrainian woman why her people liked Scrat so much. Her reply could be stitched on the flag of Ukraine: "He teaches children that life is hopeless."

Scrat is also the first star that greets you when you enter my favorite Kyiv attraction: the Muzeum of Wax Persons. Wax celebrities have careers just like professional baseball players—the very best wind up in the majors, the Madame Tussauds in large cities around the globe. When a star loses his luster through time (Arnold Schwarzenegger) or scandal (Arnold Schwarzenegger), he'll be sent off to the minors—small-town, off-brand wax museums. Arnold might even be painted green and presented as the Incredible Hulk. This kind of repurposing goes on all the time: Anne Heche becomes David Spade becomes Justin Bieber. My friend swears he saw a wax James Madison, our shortest President, redressed as Peter Pan. To make things sadder, wax figures tend to turn brown over time, so that even a Gwyneth Paltrow will take on an Afro-Caribbean complexion. All these indignities were on display in Kyiv's wax museum, filled with unrecognizable celebrities, shameless reworkings (the Cryptkeeper from *Tales from the Crypt* was dressed and labeled "Michael Jackson"), and weird cast-offs from other museums: the Freak who Could Fit a Videotape in His Mouth and the Man with the Really Bad Haircut. But my favorite attraction in the museum was not a wax figure, but a sign on the wall. Next to a sculpture that could have been any bald celebrity from Dwight Eisenhower to Charlie Brown, was a placard reading—and I'm quoting here verbatim:

"BRUCE WILLIS: From the middle of the eightieth years, Bruce tried to force one's way vainly through the upstairs. He had to play quite a bit by notable roles in the films of category of "B" and publicity rollers. He by chance was worn out in a studio tests in the 'pilot' issue of serial "Moonlight", after which he woke up a {star}. And with an output on the screens of "Die hard" the career of Bruce Willis shot up to the extraordinary heights. Psychological thriller "Sixth sense" became one of cashdesk in America, comedy The whole Nine yards also declared itself not bad."

I was starting to love Ukraine—its beauty, its boobs, its booboos—when my travel agent called with bad news: Chernobyl would be closed for the month. It wasn't a safety issue—there was a property dispute with a farmer whose fields you had to cross to get to the power plant's wreckage. Plutonium did not rattle the tour operators half as much as an angry farmer with a pitchfork. (TRAVEL TIP: Don't buy produce from a farm next to Chernobyl. Unless you get a really good price.)

I had to break the news to my wife, the words no husband should ever have to say: "Honey, I can't take you to Chernobyl."

What followed was the second-biggest meltdown in Ukrainian history. B

DAYBREAK AND A CANDLE-END

It's systemic • ***By Ron Barrett***

B

HERMETTE WIRELESS

Don't call us and we won't call you.

Be unreachable! Never be put on hold again! No 5G!

It never needs charging!

Always be out of reach!

Blame the crappy service at Hermette Wireless!

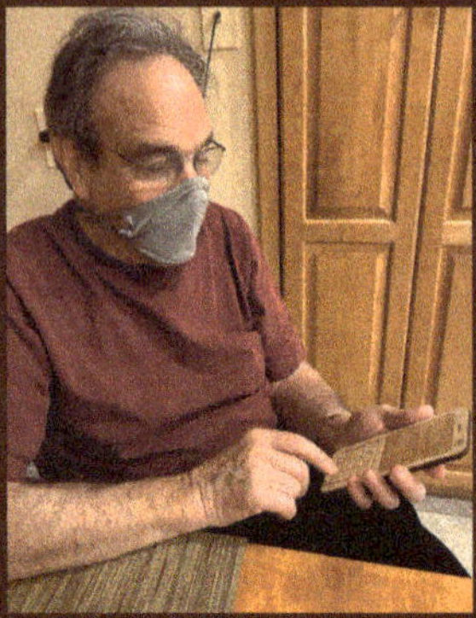

"I save hundreds of dollars on data! Just...wow!" -Ira M.

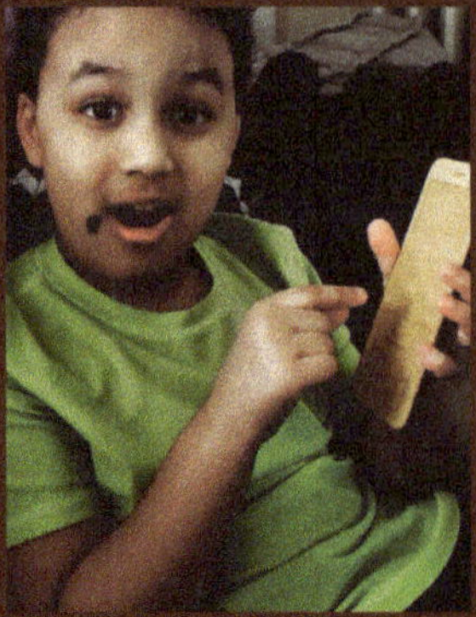

"My kids were always staring at their phones. Now they stare at me! Thanks!" -Jackie L.

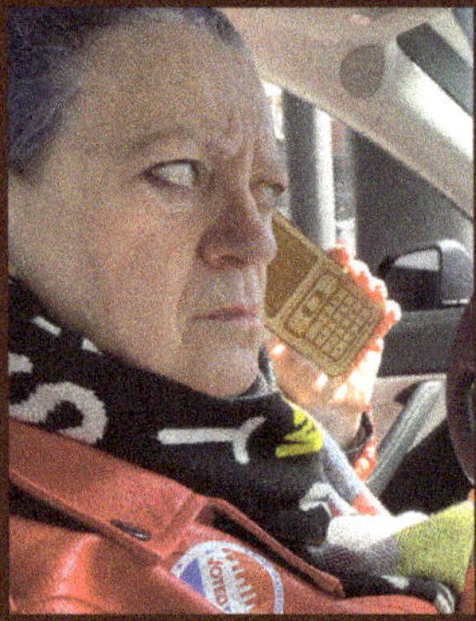

"I maximized my hermit lifestyle. It literally doesn't work anywhere!" -Laurie R.

"World's best burner phone. Perfect for camping!" -Susan H.

The leave-me-alone wooden phone!

Get the latest phone from Hermette Wireless... a phone-shaped hunk of wood that gets zero reception no matter where you are. Our phones are handmade of solid reclaimed wood. Each one is different and none of them work. Your phone does not get Twitter, Facebook, Instagram or Parler. You won't get texts, calls or emails. No meditation apps. No productivity apps. No apps at all. No podcasts. No maps. No games. No camera. Nothing. Perfect for curmudgeonly seniors. Tweens love it too! Simple to use. You just carry it around and stroke it to calm yourself down. Stop doomscrolling and start self-soothing with the hardwood quality that comes from Hermette.

Don't follow us.
@hermettewireless

Order yours today! Exclusively at: www.hermettewireless.com

This is a real product. Supplies are limited, order today.

P.S. MUELLER THINKS LIKE THIS

The cartoonist/broadcaster/writer is always walking around, looking at stuff • **By P.S. Mueller**

Sinatra In My Garage

Late one summer night in 1993, I opened the side door to my garage to find Frank Sinatra lounging with relaxed elegance in a bent lawn chair. I was struck by this. A bottle of expensive scotch sat on the lawn mower next to him. He gestured with his glass.

"Hey pally, you got some ice handy?"

I had ice. And for the next four years at precisely 11:45 p.m. each night I slipped out to my garage to hand a tumbler of ice to a living legend, who, for reasons I will never understand, found quiet pleasure in semiretirement among my collection of broken screens, dead car batteries, and garden tools. I often lingered briefly to chat, but not so long as to disturb Mr. Sinatra's solace or incite curiosity on the part of my wife. She never was a fan.

Sometime in early 1996 he asked me call him Frank. I remember that night well as I had been lugging a dead television set all the way from our basement and Mr. Sinatra, uh, Frank, opened the door for me. It was the first time I had ever seen him on his feet. (He was a little guy. A tiny old crooner he was.) I went back into the house to get his ice and returned to find him reclining once again with his feet up on an old pine Fauerbach beer case I had brought down from the attic.

Every once in a while Frank had a guest, often an old friend in show business. Dean Martin was visiting when I checked in on Frank one evening and sent me off on an errand to purchase cocktail weenies. He ate the whole jar right there in front of the both of us. And the funny thing is he insisted on a fresh toothpick for each sausage. The floor was littered with them.

I never saw her, but I swear I once heard Liza Minelli's unmistakable laugh echoing through the neighborhood at three in the morning. Joey Bishop came by, too, and sat with Frank for several hours four nights in a row without uttering a word. I didn't hang around because the pained expression on his face wore me out like an exhausting drive to Chicago. Then Chevy Chase stopped in and interrupted a story Frank was telling me about a Kansas wheat farmer he bunked with outside of Topeka in 1991. Irritated, Frank latched onto Chevy's tie, laid a Muhammad Ali anchor punch on him, and sent him packing. After that, no more guests.

Frank Sinatra left my garage in 1997. No explanation and no thanks for all the ice. A few months later I read his obituary in *The New York Times*. Not long after that a possum moved into the garage, and, for all I know, still lives there. The possum didn't seem to need any ice, so I left well enough alone until we moved and sold the place last year.

In 2002 I had a small part in a movie with Chevy Chase. I played a morgue worker and he played a dead congressman or something. I was in the dressing room when he arrived on the set, and when we were introduced, he looked right through me, as if we had never met, as if he had never in his wildest dreams expected to encounter me again and therefore hadn't. I felt no need to press the issue.

We Never Expected

We never expected pygmy Buffalo
The size of house cats. Not at all.
Tiny hooves aerating the prairie
Soil and summoning devils from the
dust, the devils
That drive in windy spirals from west
to east.
We never expected champion gazelles,
Or semisolid non-non-pixilated
creatures of the deep.
We hoard those things and save them
for another day
which may yet come this way but just
in case, we'll lock a pixel in a case,
Right next to the vase. Oh yes, we'll find
a place. **B**

P.S. MUELLER is Staff Liar of *The American Bystander.*

Are you an Introvert?

TAKE THE TEST AND FIND OUT!

DIAGNOSTICS: 0-5 SHY, 6-10 SELF COMMIT TO BEHAVIORAL HEALTH UNIT